Jersey Brew

The story of beer in New Jersey

*from our early breweries, to Prohibition gangsters,
to the breweries of today . . .*

By
Michael Pellegrino

ISBN: 978-0-9765233-1-4

Library of Congress Control Number: 2009934385

Published by *Lake Neepaulin Publishing*.
Printed in the United States of America.

Dedication

This book is dedicated to everyone with whom I have shared good beer and good conversation.

I thank my wife Jennifer and my friend James Shamah for their assistance in researching this book. I also thank the following people and organizations which contributed information and images for this book:

Mark Benbow	Beer can collection
Robert "Bruce" Mobley	Collection of embossed bottles, www.brucemobley.com
Phil Cohen	Camden Brewery images and information
www.beercans.org	Beer can collection
Scott Walker	Historian of the Orange Brewery
Glen G. Geisheimer	www.oldnewark.com

Jersey Summer Breakfast Ale by
Cricket Hill Brewery in Fairfield.

Table of Contents

Protestors picketing against Prohibition in Newark.

1 | Tapping a Jersey Brew

WHAT COULD BE BETTER THAN A BOOK ABOUT BEER, GANGSTERS, AND New Jersey? The history of beer in New Jersey is rich with colorful stories of mobsters, early breweries, corrupt politicians, and our State's fierce resistance to Prohibition.

Our earliest settlers came from European cities where the water could not be trusted, so "table beer" was the primary family beverage. Although the colonists found New Jersey's water to be pure, beer continued to be a main staple in homes. Most families brewed their own beer, and the task typically fell to the women. Households typically brewed a "table" or "small" beer and a full-strength "heavy" beer. The table beer was the family's all-purpose beverage. It had a lower alcohol level and was often sweetened with fruit. The full-bodied heavy beer was for the man of the house and for entertaining guests.

There are many great beer stories in New Jersey's history. Most of this history has remained untapped because they don't teach this stuff in school. Our earliest documented commercial brewery (in Hoboken) quickly met a violent end at the hands of Lenni Lenape Indians. Later, beer smuggling gangsters with names like Longy, Waxey, and Richie the Boot made millions brewing and distributing illegal beer during Prohibition. Mob bosses fought the Newark Beer War and they organized themselves at the first national *Meeting of Bosses* in Atlantic City. Retired Army Colonel Ira L. Reeves was appointed as New Jersey's

Prohibition Czar, only to quit after just eight months, calling for an end to Prohibition. Krueger's Brewery of Newark was the first to sell beer in cans, and Ballantine was the country's most popular ale.

Krueger's Brewery of Newark was the first to sell beer in cans.

Ballantine was one of the top breweries in the nation and sold more ale than any other brewery.

Jersey beer barons such as Wiedenmayer, Krueger, Ballantine, Trefz, Hensler, and Feigenspan made New Jersey into a major national player in beer production before Prohibition crushed the industry. Thankfully, there is a resurgence in the local beer industry. New Jersey boasts five independent microbreweries and many local brew pubs with interesting stories and great beer. To help tell all of these stories, we've included over 100 images of labels, cans, and bottles from dozens of breweries dating from 1860 to the present.

New Jersey currently boasts five microbreweries which produce award-winning, flavorful brews: Climax, Cricket Hill, Flying Fish, River Horse, and High Point.

2 | The Importance of Beer in Early America

HERE'S TO YOUR HEALTH!

Although America's pristine streams and lakes offered clean drinking water to the early settlers, settlers from European countries were ingrained with a fear of drinking water. European streams and lakes were hopelessly contaminated by the mid-1400s so generations of commoners were raised on beer and wine. Because beer was made with boiled water and contains alcohol, it was safe from microorganisms. People of the Middle Ages, however, did not know that boiling water made it safe to drink. They simply knew that drinking water made you sick, but it was safe to drink beer and wine.

Beer was relatively easy to make from easily obtained ingredients. The ingredients of "liquid bread"—barley malt, hops, and water—could simply be stored and grown in the new settlements. When barley was in short supply, the early settlers learned to use fermented corn to make beer which was reportedly just as good. They also experimented with ingredients such as pumpkin, wheat, turnips, molasses, and walnuts, to varying degrees of success. Several of today's breweries have recently introduced some niche offerings of this type.

Europeans traveling from the Old World to settle here in the 1500s through the 1700s typically brought kegs of beer for the journey, and they built breweries as a top priority upon landing in the New World. In fact, diaries from the first pilgrims who settled at Plymouth Rock,

Massachusetts, in 1620 reveal that the *Mayflower* was stocked with beer, and they decided to settle at Plymouth Rock because their rations were running low. They had actually set out to settle at a spot which is now upstate New York, but their beer supply was running low so they anchored. As recorded by William Bradford, who was the leader of the *Mayflower's* landing party at Plymouth Rock, "We had yet some beer, butter, flesh and other victuals left, which would probably be all gone; and then we should have nothing to comfort us."

Another one of the *Mayflower's* original settlers wrote of his preference for beer over the local water: "I dare not prefer it before good beere." The Plymouth settlers considered the need for a brewery to be a top priority and they completed a brewery during the first winter of 1620–1621. It was among the first structures completed.

Beer was a key concern for early settlers throughout the New World, and of course, New Jersey was no exception. Settlers in Salem County, New Jersey, along the Delaware River were noted to have "straight away busied themselves in erecting breweries."

Beer was important for a lot of reasons. Not only did it provide a safe, clean drink, but it also provided a familiar comfort of home. The settlers traveled for months aboard dangerously small ships to settle in strange and often hostile locations. They dealt with disease, food shortages, harsh weather, and less than desirable neighbors. Many of the pilgrims fled Europe because they were outcasts, criminals, or failures. Beer provided a familiar "home style," filling comfort food. "Tastes great and *more* filling." Plus it carried an alcohol level of close to 6 percent (as opposed to the 4.2 percent alcohol level typically found in such beers as Miller or Coors today) so it provided a good buzz!

Most small settlements addressed the demand for beer through home-brewing. Larger settlements included breweries which could create enough beer for public consumption—at so-called "pubs." The existence of a brewery provided an attractive feature for new settlers. The location of a brewery was also a valuable selling point for real estate. An ad in a New Brunswick newspaper seeking buyers for a large farm included: "There is also a large new brew house… containing 22 barrels."

As the colonies grew stronger, beer continued to be important to the health and nutrition of early settlers, but it also played an important

American pub circa 1500s.

social role. The American settlers brought with them a tradition of socializing in brew pubs. With no modern conveniences such as television or even electricity, there wasn't much to do at home in the evenings. People would commonly spend their evenings in the local pub where they could stay warm, share news, and have a few beers. Then, as now, beer served as a social lubricant to raise spirits, fuel discussion, and encourage socialization.

PUB HOUSE POLITICS

England had spent enormous resources fighting with France in Europe and with the rebels in the New World. One way that it sought to replenish its depleted resources and repay its debts was by taxing and draining resources from the colonies through a law known as the Stamp Act of 1765. The new law imposed a tax on goods produced within the colonies. This, of course, went over like flat beer. The colonies had no input on how the tax would be imposed, and the tax had a big impact on the most basic aspects of life in the colonies, such as beer.

Colonial leaders such as John Hancock and Samuel Adams spent many evenings in brew pubs organizing rebels known as the Sons of Liberty who sought to resist the British oppression of the colonists. They were the earliest organizers of the American Revolution. Samuel

Adams—you may recognize the name—was a Harvard-educated 43-year-old whose grandfather owned a barley malt plant on Purchase Street in Boston. John Hancock became very rich shipping goods along the coast. Both men suffered financially from the new Stamp Tax.

Adams and Hancock often met at the Black Horse Tavern in Winchester, Massachusetts, to rally the protestors and plan resistance. The most effective protest was to organize a boycott throughout the colonies on all products that were subject to the Stamp Tax. Accordingly, consumption of taxable products dropped and the rebels hit the royal crown where it hurt the most: in the purse. England soon repealed the ill-conceived Stamp Act and replaced it with the Townsend Acts in 1768, which taxed all products imported into the colonies. This of course was a great opportunity for local brewers. Anyone who drank tea was paying tax and supporting the oppressive crown. Anyone who drank locally brewed beer, on the other hand, avoided the tax, protested the British oppression, and had a good time! Local brewers prospered.

New Jersey's governor at the time was Benjamin Franklin's son, William Franklin. Unlike his famous father, William Franklin was loyal to the crown and sought to maintain his appointed position by pleasing the British as much as possible. According to the British law, its royal troops were permitted free rations from local merchants. These free rations included four pints of small beer per day for each redcoat. Despite his Tory loyalties, even Governor Franklin crossed the British by permitting local brewers to withhold beer from British troops. He passed a State law allowing brewers to substitute other goods in the place of beer.

Redcoats seeking free beer from a colonial tavern.

Beer continued to play a role in the colonial revolution. According to Gregg Smith's book, *Beer in America*, the founding fathers drank and toasted with beer as they planned the Boston Tea Party, and as they debated and drafted the Declaration of Independence. John Adams reportedly drank a pint of porter beer with breakfast every morning of his adult life. During the Revolutionary War, beer was a daily ration to the troops. In 1775 the Continental Congress passed a resolution providing that each man in the service was entitled to one quart of beer or hard cider per day. The military also used beer as a recruitment tool. It was given away at recruitment rallies. Get 'em drunk and sign 'em up. In many ways, beer helped the colonies win their independence.

BEER BREAK: *QUOTES*

"Beer is proof that God loves us and wants us to be happy."
                                        –Benjamin Franklin

"He was a wise man who invented beer."
                                                –Plato

"All right, brain, I don't like you and you don't like me—so let's just do this and I'll get back to killing you with beer."
                                        –Homer Simpson

"This is grain, which any fool can eat, but for which the Lord intended a more divine means of consumption ... Beer!"
                        –Friar Tuck in Robin Hood, Prince of Thieves,

"I am a firm believer in the people. If given the truth, they can be depended upon to meet any national crisis. The great point is to bring them the real facts, and beer."
                                        –Abraham Lincoln

"We old folks have to find our cushions and pillows in our tankards. Strong beer is the milk of the old."
                                        –Martin Luther

"New Jersey is like a beer barrel, tapped at both ends, with all the live beer running into Philadelphia and New York."
                                        –Benjamin Franklin

Beer: Helping ugly people have sex since 1962!
                                                –Unknown

Remember "I" before "E", except in Budweiser.
                                                –Anonymous

3 | New Jersey's Earliest Breweries

IN THE VERY EARLY DAYS OF THE COLONIES THERE WERE NO PUBLIC records or licensing for breweries so it is difficult to pin down details of our first breweries. Facts can only be discovered through newspaper stories and ads.

New Jersey's first commercial brew house appears to have been in Hoboken. On January 1, 1641, a settler from Holland named Aert Tewnissen Van Patten leased land to build a "Bouwerie" in Hoboken. He cleared the land, built a home and a brew house, and stocked the farm with cattle and grain. Two years later in 1643, the local Lenni Lenape natives killed his stock, burned his home, and murdered Van Patten. It was reported that the natives did not destroy the brew house. Perhaps they wanted to use it.

It is clear that New Jersey's fertile land and plentiful fresh water provided an attractive place for early European brewers to settle. They built breweries everywhere there was a water supply and a growing population. There are records of colonial breweries in Burlington, New Brunswick, Trenton, Elizabeth, Mt. Holly, Lamberton, Newark, Hackettstown, Weehawken, and Hoboken. By 1879, New Jersey boasted fifty-eight commercial brew houses with sales totaling 519,864 barrels. Almost half of the breweries (twenty-six) were in Newark due to the abundant supply of excellent water, its proximity to the New York market, and its harbor and train routes. By 1900, there were fifty-one Jersey breweries producing 2.5 million barrels of beer per year, placing New Jersey seventh among all states in beer production.

Breweries distributed beer and ale to restaurants, taverns, public houses (pubs), and beer gardens. There aren't too many beer gardens any more. The *Biergarten* originated in Bavaria and refers to open-air courtyards where beer and food is served. While many hard-working European immigrants looked down on taverns, beer gardens were more family-friendly, with trees, gravel paths, wooden benches, and family-style food. Beer gardens were most popular in areas populated with German immigrants. Some others disapproved because the gardens were often opened on Sundays—which was taboo in America.

Men wearing hats at a beer garden in the early 1900s.

1907 postcard image of the American Garden in Atlantic City.

For more details on the very early New Jersey breweries, pick up a copy of *The Early Breweries of New Jersey* by Harry B. Weiss and Grace M. Weiss. For purposes of this book, I will highlight only New Jersey's larger, better-known breweries.

Vintage Ballantine poster explaining the trademark rings.

BALLANTINE BREWERY, NEWARK, 1840

Newark's Ballantine Brewery is well remembered for its famous three-ring (pretzel shaped) logo. Contrary to "the pretzel theory," the three rings actually stand for "Purity, Body, and Flavor." Founder, Peter Ballantine got the idea for the symbol from the water marks that wet beer bottles left on a table. The ring logo was first introduced in 1879.

Ballantine was the largest of New Jersey's early brewers. Peter Ballantine emigrated from Scotland and began brewing in Albany, New York, in 1820. He relocated to Newark in 1840, and he leased a brewery which had been established by General John N. Cumming in 1805. The brewery stood at 15 High Street and was originally known as the Newark Brewery, and then as High Street Brewery. Ballantine was an industry giant for a period of time. In the 1880s Ballantine had annual sales of $750,000 and 200 employees.

Vintage Ballantine poster.

Cardboard coasters were distributed to bars to promote the brand.

After an exceptionally long run of success, in 1933 the Ballantine family sold the business to Carl and Otto Badenhausen. The Badenhausen brothers continued to grow the brand through the 1940s and 1950s with aggressive advertising. Ballantine's bottle openers, key rings, coasters, and wall clocks are widely available to collectors today.

Through its marketing and flavorful ale, Ballantine grew to be one of the top two or three brewers in the U.S. and one of the largest privately held corporations. Ballantine was the first television sponsor of the New York Yankees. The brewery sponsored radio and television broadcasts from the 1940s to the 1960s. As part of the sponsorship deal, Yankees announcers (including the legendary Mel Allen) branded Yankee home runs as "Ballantine Blasts." You can still buy an ice cold Ballantine Ale at the new Yankee Stadium for just $9!

Pint can of Ballantine beer.

Ballantine was most famous for being "America's best selling ale" but it also marketed a lager, porter, stout, and a highly regarded India Pale Ale. Its special production Burton Ale is legendary. Burton Ale was never commercially sold. It was brewed in small batches from the 1920s–1950s and aged in oak kegs for ten to twenty years, resulting in a very strong barleywine style which was given as a holiday gift to key employees, distributors, and friends of the brewery. Each bottle was dated and labeled as "Special Brew: Not For Sale" and the label had a space for the name of the person who it was "Brewed especially for" with the words, "Seasons Greetings from all of us at Ballantine." Burton Ale was brewed with a higher alcohol level (10–11 percent) and loads of hops to help preserve it during the long aging process.

SPECIAL BREW · NOT FOR SALE

BALLANTINE BURTON ALE

★

BREWED
ESPECIALLY
FOR

ON MAY 12, 1946
BOTTLED NOVEMBER 1963

PURITY BODY

FLAVOR

★   ★

Christmas Greetings from

Carlos Badenhausen
President

Otto A. Badenhausen
Vice President

Ballantine's Burton Ale—"the Holy Grail of Ale."

Unopened bottles can still be found among collectors, but at over sixty years old, they are reportedly well past their prime. From time to time they are offered on internet auction sites for over $100 per unopened bottle.

Ballantine gained heroic status among thirsty New Yorkers in 1949 by trucking in cold beer to the dry city. Brewery workers throughout New York had gone on strike. They shut down New York's thirteen brewers and they picketed the bridges, tunnels, and ferries, effectively closing New York's beer taps. Within a week, taverns and restaurants throughout the city ran dry and were laying off employees. Fearing public resentment, and in order to increase pressure on New York's strike-bound breweries, the labor union invited Ballantine to begin deliveries into the city.

Despite the union's invitation, Ballantine initially declined, explaining that it "cannot expose our drivers to violence they are bound to meet." Even though the unions guaranteed the safety of Ballantine's drivers, the company explained "No union leaders or other spokesmen on either side of the river can speak for the rank and file, as we know from experience. We have listened to these assurances before, to our sorrow."

Ballantine was understandably reluctant based on its experience a year earlier, in October of 1948 when it tried to cross a strike by New York beer truckers. Despite receiving assurances from New York police, thirty trucks were forced to return fully loaded, and Ballantine only delivered 25 percent of the beer that it attempted to ship to the city.

After receiving additional assurances from both union leaders and police officials, Ballantine and another of Newark's leading breweries, Kruegers, agreed to begin deliveries on April 15, 1949, "in order to prevent further layoffs" at pubs and restaurants. Ten thousand barrels of New Jersey beer were successfully delivered to the thirsty patrons patiently waiting in New York's pubs and restaurants. New York's breweries apparently did not want their customers to get used to drinking Jersey brew, so the strike was quickly settled. The main dispute was over the union's demand for a salary increase of $8.50 *per week* … the cost of a single beer at a Giants game today.

By the mid-1960s, Ballantine began losing popularity. In 1965 the Badenhausen family sold the company. The breweries were closed, but the brands were still marketed by Falstaff Brewing. Pabst acquired the brand in 2005 and outsources production to the Miller Brewing Company, but the present version of Ballantine ale reportedly has very little resemblance to the original best selling ale of the early 1900s.

Ballantine ad.

TREFZ BREWERY, NEWARK, 1850s–1920

One of our larger early breweries was Charles Trefz's brewery which was located between South Orange and Springfield Avenues in Newark. It was opened in the 1850s and was sold to Krueger's Brewery in 1920. Charles Trefz settled here from Germany and eventually served as a State Senator. His brewery made headlines in 1889 when it collapsed, sending a river of beer down the neighborhood streets and into basements of neighboring houses. Early reports claimed that the "river of beer" was caused by an explosion in the brewery, but it was later determined that the enormous weight of two vats of beer on the third floor was simply too great for the floor beams to carry. The vats crashed through two floors causing $90,000 of damage: $75,000 in beer and $15,000 to rebuild the brew house.

RIVERS OF JERSEY BEER.

A NEWARK BREWERY EXPLODES, CAUSING A LOSS OF $100,000.

Charles Trefz's brewery, on Rankin-street, between South Orange and Springfield avenues, Newark, was partially wrecked yesterday by a remarkable accident. The resting and fermenting departments of the brewery are in a three-story brick building facing on Rankin-street. It contained a score or more of great vats filled with thousands of gallons of beer. All the floors of the building were cooled with ammonia pipes running to an ice machine.

Between 12 and 1 o'clock yesterday the neighborhood was startled by a terrific explosion in this building. The heavy walls trembled as though shaken by an earthquake. Then beer began to gush in streams from the rear windows, and it kept on gushing into the street until it rose above the level of the sidewalks and poured into the basements of the neighboring houses. The atmosphere became suddenly so charged with ammonia that people withdrew from the streets.

The explosion will probably always remain a mystery. One of the ammonia pipes forming part of the patent ice machine is believed to have sprung a leak, and the gas, escaping into the cold air of the building, expanded and caused the explosion. The power of its expansion was sufficient to force the walls apart, and the floors, loosened from their supports, fell, with the great vats which rested upon them, to the ground. The walls of the building were so badly shattered that they will in all probability have to be torn down. There is danger of the great north wall falling upon a little dwelling house which adjoins it and crushing it into kindling wood.

The brewery is under the supervision of Charles Trefz, who has just been elected to succeed Frank McDermitt as a member of the Assembly. He is now in the West on business. It is stated that the loss will reach $100,000. No lives were lost.

The New York Times
Published: December 3, 1889
Copyright © The New York Times

New York Times article, December 3, 1889.

KRUEGER'S BREWERY, NEWARK, 1858–1961

Sixteen-year-old Gottfried Krueger was summoned from Germany in 1854, to help his uncle, John Laible, run a small brewery in Newark. Gottfried traveled to America and learned the beer-making business as an apprentice. By1865, Krueger, his Uncle Laible, and a brewer named Gottlieb Hill bought a brewery and renamed their business the Hill and Krueger Brewery. The partners aggressively expanded, and by 1875 their production had increased to almost 25,000 barrels a year. Gottfried soon bought out his partners and became the sole owner of the G. Krueger Brewing Company.

Krueger was making millions and he continued to expand through mergers and acquisitions of other breweries including the Trefz Brewery, Albany Brewing, Lyons and Sons Brewery, Home Brewery, and Union Brewery. The combined breweries could produce 500,000 barrels of beer per year for Krueger.

In 1888, Krueger spent $250,000 on the most lavish mansion ever built in Newark, located on High Street. All of Newark's beer barons seemed to feel a civic duty, and Krueger was no exception. He served as a lay judge for eleven years; he was elected as a county freeholder, and also served as a Newark city council member.

Early Krueger embossed bottle with rustic beer mug design. These bottles were typically used in bars and restaurants and were returned to the brewery to be refilled.

Amber bottles preserve the beer   Each bottle was embossed by
by shielding it from light.   hand so they varied slightly.

In May 1914, Gottfried Krueger and his wife Bertha set sail for
Germany on a trip back to their homeland. Unfortunately, World
War I broke out soon thereafter and they were trapped inside Germany
for several years. Luckily, beer continued to flow from Krueger's brewery
in his absence.

When Prohibition hit the industry in 1920, Krueger was forced
to sell off all of his breweries except his original facility at 75 Belmont
Avenue. Although he had already made an enormous fortune, he
struggled to remain in business through the dry years by selling soda and
low-alcohol beer. Gottfried Krueger died in 1926 before Prohibition
ended, and his son William Krueger took over.

When Prohibition finally ended on March 22, 1933, Krueger's was
ready. It was the only brewery in New Jersey ready to begin selling
beer immediately. Krueger's sold beer by the cup right from its brewery
doors, and newspapers reported that it took two days to restore order in
front of the brewery.

Krueger's was also ready to lead the industry in marketing. In 1934
it was the first company in the world to sell beer in cans (as detailed

in chapter 7). By the late 1930s Krueger's dropped the "s" and became Krueger Beer. It continued to grow through the 1940s and became one of the biggest breweries in the East. By 1952 Krueger was brewing one million barrels of beer per year.

Krueger beer can without the "s."

Krueger can with the large K-man.

Krueger often changed the color and design of its cans but maintained the K-man logo.

Krueger's is a favorite among collectors of beer memorabilia because it was extremely active in advertising. It continually churned out new and different ads and marketing pieces such as coasters, can openers, etc. Bottle labels and beer cans were redesigned almost every year. The "K-man" became a well-known symbol of the brand.

The K-man was included on Krueger's history-making first beer can, and he was included in the giant neon light that was built in 1937 at Krueger's Brewery in Newark. The sign was fifty-seven feet tall and fifty feet wide, topped by a K-man standing over two stories tall.

In 1958 Krueger celebrated its 100th anniversary, but it was losing market share to national companies like Anheuser-Busch. In 1961 the company was sold, and the original facility in Newark was redeveloped as a shopping center.

CHRISTIAN FEIGENSPAN BREWING COMPANY, NEWARK, 1875

The Christian Feigenspan Brewing Company was founded 1875, and named after the founder and his son. There were four other large breweries in Newark at that time (Wiedenmayer, Krueger, Ballantine's, and Hensler's) but Feigenspan tried to set himself apart and show his Newark pride by printing PON ("Pride of Newark") on his bottles and cans.

Christian Feigenspan Jr. (1876–1939) assumed control of the family brewery in 1899, upon the death of his father. Like many other brew masters of this time, the Feigenspans were involved in civic affairs. Feigenspan served on the so-called "Committee of 100" to celebrate Newark's 250th anniversary in 1916, and he paid $70,000 to sponsor the Venetian Colleoni sculpture which still rests in Lincoln Park.

PON can.

Feigenspan's PON—the "Pride of Newark."

Christian Feigenspan P.O.N. Advertisement.

Like other breweries, Feigenspan was crushed by the onset of Prohibition. The brewery began to produce legal, low-alcohol "near" beer, but there was very low demand and it was not a profitable venture. As president of the United States Brewers' Association, he led a suit in 1920 seeking a court ruling that Prohibition was unconstitutional. Feigenspan argued that the amendment was not applicable in New Jersey because our State did not ratify it. He also argued that his beer was not intoxicating! He lost.

Feigenspan again made news in 1927 when he opened twenty-six vats of pre-Prohibition beer, allowing the "real" beer to spill into the Passaic River. Feigenspan had petitioned the Court to allow him to give the beer away to his shareholders, but he was denied, so he opened the valves and watched 300,000 gallons of his beloved brew go to waste.

WIEDENMAYER BREWING COMPANY, NEWARK, 1848–1920

George Wiedenmayer was born in Newark in 1848, and he started in the beer business in 1870 with his father (former Newark mayor), Christian Wiedenmayer. George was elected to serve as a State Assemblyman, and he later owned two steam boat lines in Newark. The brewery reached a peak of 75,000 barrels per year.

Prohibition drove the Wiedenmayers out of brewing and into the ice cream business in 1920. In 2005 the company resurrected the old family recipe. Wiedenmayer Jersey Lager is offered by the Wiedenmayer

Horse drawn beer wagon.

Brewing Company, located in Bedminster, New Jersey, but it is contract brewed by Olde Saratoga Brewing (Mendocino Brewing) in Saratoga Springs, New York.

HENSLER BREWERY, NEWARK, 1860–1958

The Joseph Hensler Brewing Company of Newark, one of Newark's Big Five, was located at 73 Hamburg Place (now Wilson Avenue) in the Ironbound Section of Newark. Brew master Joseph Hensler began to master his trade in 1850 while working at Lorenz and Jacquillard Brewery. He started his own brewery in 1860 and the brewery operated for almost 100 years through 1958.

Hensler ad for light beer directed at women.

This Hensler beer bottle was embossed
with a relatively simple design.

It was alleged that mobster Waxey Gordon and his partners controlled
the brewery during Prohibition. Hensler built a family mansion at
426 Lafayette Street, right across the street from the brewery. It still
stands today as a funeral home.

FRIELINGHAUS-LYON & SONS BREWERY, NEWARK, 1864

Another brewery operated on South Canal Street in Newark in the
late 1800s. It was initially owned by Jacob Leonhart, and the 1860 New
Jersey Business Census indicates that it was taken over by the Rumpf
& Frielinghaus Brewing Company. Mr. D.M. Lyon bought the brewery
in 1864 and operated as Lyon & Sons Brewery. It was later absorbed by
Krueger's.

Lyon & Sons wire cap bottle with a detailed lion's head design. Wire caps were common before the pop-off crown caps were developed.

This simpler Lyon & Sons bottle without the lion logo was "not to be sold" to individuals. Bottles with simpler designs were typically used by bars and restaurants.

ANHEUSER-BUSCH, NEWARK, 1951

Newark is also the site of Anheuser-Busch's first plant outside of St. Louis. It opened in 1951 and today this brewery produces more Budweiser than any other plant in the world. Budweiser and Michelob are Americanized versions of pilsner style lagers—which is the most popular type of beer in the world. Budweiser appears to be named after a town which had been known as Budweis in the Czech Republic where Pilsner style beer originated.

Postcard from the 1960s of the Anheuser-Busch plant on Route 1 in Newark which brewed Budweiser and Michelob.

Familiar Bud can.

GREENVILLE BREWING/COLUMBIA BREWING COMPANY, JERSEY CITY, 1890–1920

The Greenville Brewing Company opened at 235 Bartholdi Avenue in the Greenville (Southern) neighborhood of Jersey City in 1890. Its founders, Charles Ferger, Adolph Becker, and Daniel Kohl brewed German style ales. The brewery changed hands and became known as the Columbia Brewing Company in 1905 and continued operations until it was shut down by Prohibition in 1920.

LEMBECK AND BETZ EAGLE BREWING, JERSEY CITY, 1869–1920

The Lembeck and Betz Eagle Brewing Company was founded in downtown Jersey City in 1869 by Henry B. Lembeck and John F. Betz. The brew house took up an entire block between Ninth and Tenth streets, and Grove (Manila Avenue) and Henderson (Marin Boulevard)

Greenville bottle with wire cap and beer barrel logo.

Exceptional detail for an embossed glass bottle.

Lembeck and Betz
Eagle Brewing bottle.   Eagle bottle.   Eagle Brewing bottle.

streets. The brewery initially produced English style pale ale and porter, and then began to brew lager in 1889 to meet demand of the influx of Germans into the area. To meet growing demand, Lembeck merged with the Eagle Brewing Company of Newark.

The business grew to become the fourth largest brewery in New Jersey, distributing 250,000 barrels per year at its peak. The brewery closed during Prohibition, and the facility was sold and converted into a refrigeration plant. In 1984, the area was designated as the Lembeck and Betz Eagle Brewing Company District on the National Register of Historic Places. The brewery buildings were demolished in 1997 and a school is now located on the site.

Lembeck was an active community leader in the Greenville section of Jersey City. He acquired and developed blocks of land and he was a founder of the Greenville Banking and Trust Company, then became vice president of the Third National Bank of Jersey City. He built a mansion at 46

The Lembeck Mansion as it appears today at the corner of Lembeck Avenue and Old Bergen Road in Jersey City.

Columbia Place (today Lembeck Avenue) and Old Bergen Road. Lembeck died in 1904 and his wife eventually donated the Lembeck mansion to St. Anne's Home for the Aged (which is now part of the York Street Project).

SPRATTLER AND MENNEL BREWERY, PATERSON, 1870–1941

Sprattler and Mennel Brewery was opened in 1870 on Marshall Street, in Paterson. They leased the facility from the Braun Brewery which had operated at that site since 1855. The brewery was sold to an English conglomerate in July of 1889 along with Paterson's other large breweries of that time—Katz Brothers, Hinchliffe Brothers, and Christian Braun breweries. The Sprattler Brewery closed during Prohibition until gangster Waxey Gordon bought it and began smuggling real beer out of the brewery through fire hoses that he ran along the underground sewer pipes. Waxey Gordon is discussed further in chapter 6.

The Peter Breidt Brewery circa 1882.

BREIDT BREWING COMPANY, ELIZABETH, 1867

The Peter Breidt Brewing Company was based in Elizabeth, New Jersey, on Pearl Street from 1867 to 1951. Peter Breidt died May 10. 1904, but the company continued on. The Elizabeth High School now occupies this site.

Breidt Brewing was involved in the Great New Jersey Beer Bribery Plot along with the Rising Sun Brewery and Hygeia Brewing Companies in 1923.

Newspaper headlines blared "Eleven Arrested in Plot to Flood New York with Jersey Beer." Prohibition had shut down most breweries, but these breweries survived by supposedly converting their beer into

Rising Sun Brewery bottle.

Hygeia Brewing bottle.

low-alcohol near beer. Very few people would drink that stuff, so these breweries quietly sold normal full-alcohol beer through the black market.

The 1923 arrests were big news. Not only were these three breweries involved, but indictments were also issued against bootleggers, a federal Prohibition agent, and four New Jersey state officials. The indictments alleged that over $800,000 had been paid in bribes to enforcement officials to look the other way and allow the breweries and traffickers to smuggle illegal Jersey beer into New York. The plot included efforts to crack down on rival bootleggers from Pennsylvania who also were trying to sneak beer into the lucrative New York market. The smugglers were provided with protection for beer runs into the city, and in exchange the indicted State and federal officials were alleged to have received hundreds of thousands of dollars in cash, automobiles, and even World Series tickets.

Newspaper articles included specific details of the alleged corruption and payoffs. The feds had an undercover agent in place who witnessed the bribes and protection scheme, and 125 barrels of beer were recovered. The evidence seemed to be clear and overwhelming. As reported by the *New York Times* on October 19, 1923:

> The scheme of "protection" worked well and Jersey foam was quenching the thirsty in September (1923) in many saloons, restaurants and speakeasies in the metropolitan district. The "corrupted" agents and the brewers ... entertained each other right royally at the weekly business meetings when reports showing the spread of Jersey beer and the complete evaporation of Pennsylvania [beer] were delivered.

Despite what appeared to be abundant solid evidence, and numerous stories in the press, all of the major indictments were suddenly dismissed on August 30, 1926. The dismissal papers which the federal prosecutor filed in court explained that the indictments were based on evidence obtained by undercover agent Saul Grill who had simply "disappeared." The government believed "it could not obtain a conviction without his testimony."

HUDSON COUNTY CONSUMERS BREWING COMPANY, UNION CITY, 1902–1928

The buildings at 481–515 Summit Avenue in Union City are the site of what was The Hudson County Consumers Brewing Company. The long-named company was formed in 1899 and began selling beer in 1902. This part of Union City was known as West Hoboken back then. The brewery thrived until Prohibition. It finally closed in late 1928 and the property was acquired by the city in the early 1930s. Roosevelt Stadium was then built on the site so the beer connection continued until the stadium was demolished in 2005 to clear space for the new $136 million Union City High School and Union City Athletic Complex.

THE ORANGE BREWING COMPANY, ORANGE, 1902

Michael Winter and his brothers, Wolfgang and Aloysius, came to America from Bayern, Germany, in 1873, and began brewing beer in Pittsburgh,

Pennsylvania, under the name of The M. Winter Brothers Brewing Company. In 1899 they sold the brewery to the Pittsburgh Brewing Company.

In 1901 the Winter Brothers moved to Orange, New Jersey, and started construction on The Orange Brewing Company on the corner of Hill and Prince streets in Orange. The whole facility was built for just $350,000.

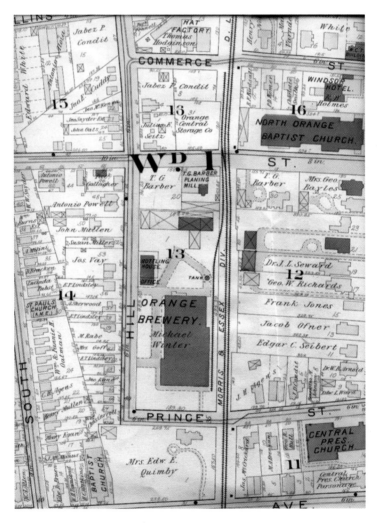

A 1904 map of the new
Orange Brewery complex.

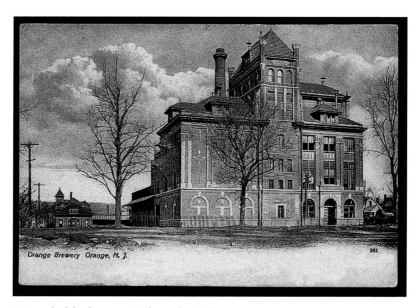

Postcard of the brewery in the early 1900s.

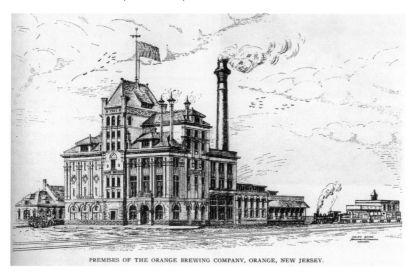

PREMISES OF THE ORANGE BREWING COMPANY, ORANGE, NEW JERSEY.

A 1902 sketch of the brewery.

The huge brewery produced 100,000 barrels per year of pilsner beer, an ale, a porter, and another recipe for export only. The beer was

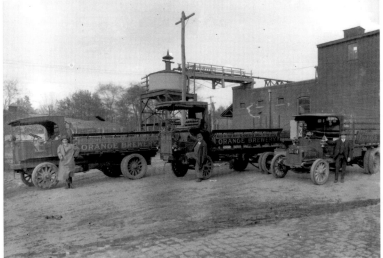

Orange Brewery's delivery trucks.

initially distributed to local taverns and even to homes by horse-drawn wagons. The brewery later used trucks.

Like many other breweries, the onset of Prohibition crushed the Winter brothers and the Orange Brewery ceased by 1920 after twenty

Embossed bottle with "Purity & Strength"
slogan inside a circle of chain.

years of brewing Jersey beer. At first the Winter brothers converted
the Orange Brewery for production of soda, but after a few years, the
brewery was sold in 1925.

The brewery fell into the wrong hands, and in October of 1927, the
new owners were indicted for distributing illegal beer to destinations as
far away as Kansas City. The beer was smuggled in containers marked as
"paint," "oils," and "boiler compound."

Prohibition finally ended in 1933 and beer began to flow legally again.
The Orange Brewery was purchased by John F. Trommers Breweries
of Brooklyn, New York, for $700,000. The facility was renovated to
increase capacity to 300,000 barrels per year, and Trommers continued
to brew beer at the Orange location throughout the 1930s and 1940s.

In November, 1950, the facility was sold to Liebmann Breweries
of New York, which bottled Rheingold Beer at the Orange facility up
until the 1970s. Demand for Rheingold continued to sag so the brand

119 HILL STREET
ORANGE, NEW JERSEY
PHONE ORANGE 5-4100

Postcard depicting the expanded Trommers facility in Orange.

Can of Trommer's beer "of New Jersey."

and the Orange brewery was passed through various owners until it was finally closed in 1980. The plant has since been completely demolished after seventy-eight years of operation.

CAMDEN COUNTY BEVERAGE COMPANY, CAMDEN, 1910: "NONE BETTER"

Camden's brewery was located at Fillmore and Bulson streets from 1910 through the 1960s. It drew its water supply from Camden's artesian wells and boasted that its water was considered "among the best in the United States, and certainly in this part of the East," according to a U.S. Geological Survey in 1927.

The brewery was known as the Camden City Brewery when it was first opened in 1910 by F.A. Poth & Sons, Inc., a Philadelphia-based brewery.

As discussed in further detail in chapter 6, Max Hassel, "the Gentleman Beer Baron," acquired the brewery in 1928 and operated under the name Camden County Beverage Company. The brewery

Wire cap Poth & Sons embossed bottle.

came under the control of Mickey "The Muscle" Duffy who was a strong-arm Philadelphia gangster, and it was a major source of illegal beer during Prohibition.

When Prohibition was repealed, legitimate owners took over and continued brewing as the Camden County Beverage Company, with Fred A. Martin as president. From those days through the 1960s, the Camden County Beverage Company brewed and bottled Camden Lager Beer, Lord Camden Ale, Camden Bock Beer, and Cerveza Bohio in Camden.

Camden's slogan, "None Better" appeared on the majority of its ads and even on some labels.

Camden Bock label.

The Camden Lager label looked a lot like a Bud.

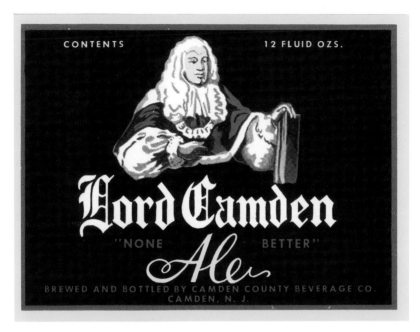

Lord Camden Ale label.

"Lord Camden" was the title held by Charles Pratt, the highest-ranking British government official who publicly and persistently protested the British Crown's actions against the Colonies. Although he was a British official, he was considered to be a hero of the American Revolution. By the end of the late 1700s, 26 American cities and towns were named in his honor. Camden, N.J., is the largest.

After the brewery closed, Camden Beer continued to be sold, but it was brewed and packaged by Esslinger Brewery in Philadelphia for distribution in and around Camden.

TRENTON BREWERY/PEOPLE'S BREWING/METROPOLIS BREWERY, TRENTON, 1899

In 1891, Col. A.R. Kuser founded a brewery on the corner of Lafor and Lamberton streets in South Trenton. The brewery stood until 1998 and it is now identified as a contaminated "brownfields" site. It was first used by the Trenton Brewing Company, a Trenton-based brewing

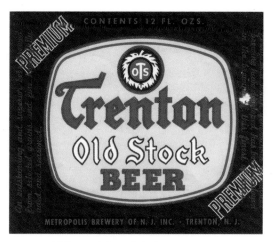

Trenton Olde Stock beer label.

People's lager beer can.

operation owned by the Kuser family. In 1899, the Kusers sold the company to People's Brewing Company which used the facility until 1949.

In 1949, the Metropolis Brewery Company, owned by Louis Hertzberg, purchased the facility and began to brew Champale at the Trenton Site. In 1972, the Hertzbergs sold the Champale label and the brewery to Iroquois Brands, Ltd. Under Iroquois's mass marketing, Champale's sales grew tremendously, but by 1981 sales began to fall. In 1986, the G. Heilman Brewing Company purchased the brands and closed the plant, leaving close to 200 workers unemployed.

During the course of its existence the brewery marketed dozens of brands including Wilco, Champale Malt Liquor, People's, Pilser's Maltcrest, A&P, Tuder, Dominion, Old Dutch, Lion, Regent, Cherry Hill, and Black Horse.

Wilco brand beer was produced in Trenton from 1967 through 1972. It was also brewed under contract by Eastern Brewery in Hammonton, New Jersey.

Old Dominion beer had a run from 1958 through 1965.

Black Horse Ale was brewed in Trenton from 1973–1987.

Old Dutch lager was produced in Trenton from 1950 through 1968.

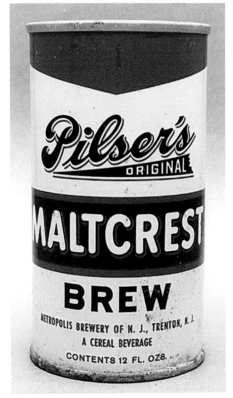

Pilser's Maltcrest brew had a short run from 1951–1956.

Remember when supermarkets sold beer? Metropolis brewed the Gilt Edge and Rialto brands marketed exclusively in Grand Union supermarkets, and it brewed the Tudor brand exclusively for A&P supermarkets, as well as Waldbaum's beer.

Gilt Edge was marketed exclusively by Grand Union supermarkets.

Rialto was also a Grand Union brand.

A&P supermarkets owned the Tudor brand.

Tudor Cream Ale was also available only at A&P.

Waldbaum's didn't even bother to create a name for its beer.

HAUCK/HARRISON BREWERY/PETER DOELGER BREWERY, HARRISON, 1844–1947

The Harrison Brewery traces its roots back to the Hauck family who were brewing beer in New York City since 1844. In 1869 the brew master's son, Peter Hauck moved the business to Harrison, New Jersey, to expand. The Harrison brewery was originally known as Hauck & Kaufman but Hauck became the sole owner by 1881 and was brewing 100,000 barrels per year by 1900. The brewery sold three lagers, Hauck's Special, Hauck's Extra, and Golden Brew, and all three labels included a distinctive large letter "H."

Peter Hauck's oldest grandson, Karl Hauck Bissel married Phoebe Doelger whose family owned a large brewery in New York. Eventually the Doelger family took over operations and operated at the Peter Doelger Brewery.

A rusty can of Peter Doelger with the slogan "priceless difference in flavor."

Prohibition caused the Doelger family to shut down, and the Harrison Brewery fell into the hands of alleged gangsters, Max Greenberg and Max Hassel (discussed in depth in chapter 6) who operated in as the Harrison Beverage Company.

When Prohibition eventually came to an end, the Peter Doelger company regained control of the brewery and rereleased their popular brands. They brewed both lagers and ales, and they introduced a so-called "Half & Half" which was an unusual combination of lager and ale.

The marketplace had changed after Prohibition, and the Doelger brewery could not compete with the giant national brands like Miller and Bud. It closed down in 1947. The city of Harrison took over the building by 1951 and razed it in 1957 to make room for a school.

HOFFMAN BREWING/PABST BREWING COMPANY, NEWARK, 1930

Pabst Blue Ribbon can.

The brewing of Pabst Blue Ribbon beer did not start here in New Jersey. Pabst was based in Milwaukee, Wisconsin, and the company ultimately purchased the defunct facility of the Hoffman Brewing Company on South Orange Avenue and Grove Street in Newark. Hoffman brewed beer, but it was best known for its soda, and it erected a giant water tower in the shape of a soda bottle that was visible from the Garden State Parkway. The sixty-foot-tall bottle was originally painted in the colors of Hoffman Ginger Ale and was the largest bottle in the world when Hoffman opened the brewery in 1930.

The bottle was 185 feet above the street and held 55,000 gallons of water. Up to six men could stand on its cap and it was made of quarter-inch copper plated steel.

When Pabst took over the plant it changed the giant bottle to resemble a bottle of PBR beer. Pabst closed the Newark plant in 1982 and sadly removed the enormous beer bottle that had become such a highly visible icon for Jersey travelers.

Sad ruins of the giant bottle.

It is said that the enormous bottle is now stored in pieces with hope that it may be restored someday. It would make a great nostalgic attraction at the Jersey Shore or at the Prudential Arena in Newark.

Notice the PBR case in the foreground.

EASTERN BREWING CORPORATION, HAMMONTON, 1933

The Eastern Brewing Company of Hammonton acquired brands of small defunct regional breweries, and it relaunched the brands to sell in specific markets. Its top brands were Colonial Brewing and Waukee Brewing which produced Topper, Milwaukee, Old German, Davidson, and Holland beer.

Colonial can, 1953–1990.

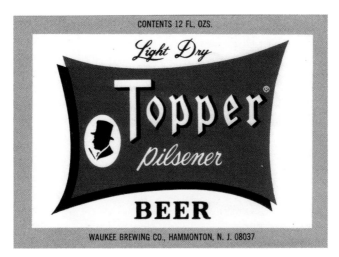

Topper was the primary brand of the Rochester Brewing
Company which dates back to 1875 in Rochester, New York.
Eastern took over the brand in the 1970s.

Old German, 1956–1990.

Holland.

Davidson's Premium, 1955–1960.

Eastern targeted the Hispanic market with its San Juan label distributed under its Cerveceria San Juan brand.

San Juan can, 1966–1975.

Old Bohemian can.

DRAFT BEER FLAVOR

IT'S STERILIZED

Old Bohemian

EASTERN BREWING CORP., HAMMONTON, N. J.

CONTENTS 12 FLUID OUNCES

FULLY AGED

BREWERY FRESH PASTEURIZED BEER
Brewed with Pure Artesian Well Water.

Old Bohemian label.

Eastern showed off its Jersey roots with brands that were specifically aimed at local residents. From 1959 through 1964, it brewed Garden State beer for Bilow discount liquor stores, and Eastern brewed and packaged Jersey Gem under its Colonial brand for Valencia Liquor Shops.

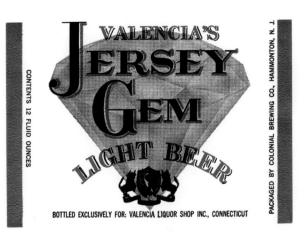

VALENCIA'S JERSEY GEM LIGHT BEER

CONTENTS 12 FLUID OUNCES

PACKAGED BY COLONIAL BREWING CO., HAMMONTON, N. J.

BOTTLED EXCLUSIVELY FOR: VALENCIA LIQUOR SHOP INC., CONNECTICUT

Jersey Gem label, 1953–1958.

Bilow Garden State cream ale,
bock beer, and light beer labels,
1959-1964

Eastern was also New Jersey's only contract brewery, producing beer for a variety of small labels which it did not own. Its best known label was Wilco Premium which was contracted by the Colonial Brewing Company in the 1970s for the Roger Wilco Liquor Store chain in and around Burlington County. It also brewed Blanchard beer for the Blanchard Liquor store chain.

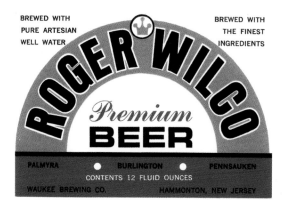

"Roger Wilco" means
"Information received;
will comply."

Blanchard's can.

Its most controversial brand was Nude Beer which it brewed for California's Golden Beverage Company. It soon halted production and sales in New Jersey because it was deemed inappropriate. The Nude Beer label could be rubbed off to reveal a nude woman.

Nude Beer label before the bikini is rubbed off.

UNITED BREWING COMPANY OF NEWARK, 1933–1938

Located at 333 Springfield Avenue, the United Brewing Company was a small brewer with local distribution of Oldburger Beer and United Ale. Its roots date back to Baier & Piez Brewery in 1874.

IMPORTED JERSEY BEER

For a period of time it was popular for breweries in other states to market their beer in New Jersey by labeling it with a "Jersey" name. Unsuspecting consumers never knew the difference. Hoboken Ale was brewed by Gold Coast Brewery in New Haven, Connecticut, Goldfinch ale (named after the New Jersey state bird) was owned by the Goldfinch Brewing Company in Mt. Laurel but was brewed by Lion Brewing Company in Wilkes Barre, Pennsylvania.

Some clever out-of-state companies sought to take advantage of the crowds that rush to the Jersey Shore every summer. Atlantic City Diving Horse Ale was distributed by the Atlantic City Brewing Company but it was brewed by Lion Brewing in Pennsylvania. LBI Wheat Beer and Avalon Amber Ale were brewed in Delaware for the now defunct Shore Brewing Company.

THE SPIRIT OF THE DIVING HORSE IS CAPTURED IN THIS CLASSIC ATLANTIC CITY BEER.

Atlantic City Diving Horse label. Diving Horse is no longer brewed in New Jersey.

Embossed wire cap bottle from Atlantic City Brewing
Company with a lighthouse image boasting "makers
of the finest beer in the United States."

Vintage Atlantic City Brewing bottle with detailed image
of lighthouse from the early 1900s when Atlantic City
Brewing Company was based in Jersey.

Contrary to its own name, after 1964, Garden State Beer was produced by the Walter Brewing Company in a far-away place called Eau Claire, Wisconsin. From 1959 to 1964 it was produced in the Garden State by Colonial Brewing Company in Hammonton.

Garden State Beer cans.

Some Jersey-named beers were actually brewed here. Mile Square (named for the mile square city of Hoboken), Camden beer and Lord Camden ale, Trenton Old Stock beer, Red Bank lager, and Feigenspan's PON (Pride of Newark) are no longer available but were brewed here in Jersey.

Camden Bock beer label.

Camden lager label.

PON—"Pride of Newark."

Roselle Park beer is brewed by the Climax Brewery in Roselle Park, Jersey Summer Breakfast Ale is a light, fruity beer by Cricket Hill Brewery in Fairfield, and Barnegat Light Beer is brewed by Basil Ts Brewery in Toms River.

Jersey Summer Breakfast Ale.

EMPTY KEGS

Unfortunately, almost all of these breweries no long exist, and most people younger than 50 never got to sample these Jersey brews. At least New Jersey still boasts six breweries and over a dozen brew pubs, so it is still possible to enjoy great beer that is brewed close to home (see chapter 9).

New Jersey's five microbreweries: High Point, Flying Fish, Climax, River Horse, and Cricket Hill.

BEER BREAK: *TOASTS*

In heaven there is no beer...
That's why we drink ours here.

For every wound, a balm
For every sorrow, cheer.
For every storm, a calm.
For every thirst, a beer.

You guys came by to have some fun.
You'll come and stay all night, I fear.
But I know how to make you run.
I'll serve you all generic beer.

Here's to women, beer and song, may none of them be flat.

MEN, start your livers!

Give a man a fish and he will eat for a day. Teach him how to fish and
he will sit in a boat and drink beer all day!

Cheers!

4 | The Bishops' Law: No Beer on Sundays

TODAY IT SEEMS TO BE AN INALIENABLE RIGHT TO HAVE A BEER (OR THREE) at a sports bar on a Sunday afternoon while watching the Giants and Jets on big screen TVs. This simple pleasure, however, wasn't always legal in our state on Sundays. Under early common law and custom, the sale of liquor was prohibited on Sundays, as all bars and pubs were supposed to be closed on Sundays. Fortunately, in the 1800s, the Sunday beer ban was largely ignored. Pubs opened, officials looked the other way, and few people complained. Things began to change toward the end of the 1900s. Religious groups began to make noise about the evil of alcohol consumption. Ultimately, the religious right sought to prohibit consumption of alcoholic beverages entirely, but as a first step clergy groups began to clamor for enforcement of the existing Sunday closure laws.

Some municipalities and counties buckled under pressure and adopted local excise laws to enforce the Sunday drinking ban, but the dry-Sunday ordinances were largely ignored. Newspaper writers took Sunday strolls from pub to pub and reported on the abundant flow of beer. *The New York Times* sent a staff writer to Washington Street in Hoboken on a Sunday in May, 1888. He reported:

> *Most of the saloons did close their front doors, but it seems a peculiarity of Hoboken saloons that nine out of ten of them are blessed with either a side door or a more or less devious means of entrance through some adjoining building.*

On a Sunday visit to Jersey City the reporter found "very many of the saloon keepers kept their side doors opened." The Jersey City police commissioner had publicly ordered that all patrolmen would be in full uniform. The saloons would simply close their side door if a uniformed officer approached. It was made clear that the local police were taking a "don't ask—don't tell" approach.

In 1906, a group of clergy from various religions made a trip to Trenton and drafted a new law. Republican Governor Casper Stokes signed the bill, and the new law became known as the Bishops' Law (in reference to the clergy's role in pushing it through). The new law imposed strict penalties for anyone serving beer on a Sunday. The barkeep could be fined up to $1,000, jailed, and lose his liquor license. The law also prohibited back rooms so that it would be more difficult to secretly break the law.

The Bishops' Law went into effect on July 8, 1906. Naturally the Sunday beer ban wasn't well received throughout New Jersey. Regardless of the strict penalties, many pubs ignored the law. Local police and borough officials continued to look the other way. Economic forces compelled bars to remain open if other competing bars remained open in the neighborhood.

By July of 1908, the open disregard for the new law was so rampant that the new governor, John F. Fort, appointed a commission to study the problem. After six weeks the Commission reported that the Bishops' Law was routinely ignored in most communities throughout the State. Only a handful of small religious communities actively enforced the ban. The Commission reported "that the Act is studiously ignored by the people, and so generally unpopular that even the officials … are afraid to act under it." Local police generally refused to enforce the law. On the few occasions when charges were filed, the jury refused to convict.

In August 1908 Governor Fort wrote an open letter to the public threatening to call in the National Guard to enforce the law if local Atlantic City officials refused to enforce the law. Atlantic City complained that its bars could not be expected to close unless all of the resort areas in southern Jersey would also comply. The National Guard was not called in, but a few years later the federal government put an end to the issue by adopting a nationwide ban on all alcoholic beverages—anywhere, any day.

The Prohibition era began.

Prohibition officers dumping illegal beer.

BEER BREAK: *TASTES GREAT OR LESS FILLING?*

Ever wonder if you are really getting the tap beer that you order at a bar? Don't count on it. Those fancy tap handles aren't always hooked up to the matching brand of beer. The New Jersey Casino Control Commission fined Resorts Atlantic City $5,000 for having mislabeled beer keg taps at one casino bar on two occasions. Beer taps labeled "Miller Lite" and "Miller Genuine Draft" were both connected to a keg containing Miller Lite. The Commission found that the Casino committed the same violation in August of 2008 when two of its taps were labeled "Coors Original" and "Coors Light," but both were dispensing the full-calorie, full-carb beer.

Alcohol content, calories, and carbohydrates in various beer brands.

Brand	Brewery	% Alcohol	Calories/ 12 oz	Carbs (grams)
Amstel Light	Amstel Brouwerij B.V. (Holland)	3.9	99	5.33
Bass Pale Ale	Bass (England)	5.5	160	13.1
Blue Moon	Adolph Coors	5.4	171	12.9
Bud Light	Anheuser Busch	4.1	110	6.5
Budweiser	Anheuser Busch	5	145	10.6
Coors	Adolph Coors	5	142	10.6
Coors Light	Adolph Coors	4.2	102	5
Corona	Cereveria Modela SA (Mexico)	4.6	148	13.99
Corona Light	Cereveria Modela SA (Mexico)	4.5	109	5
Foster's Lager	Garlton & United (Australia)	5.1	156	11
Guinness Extra Stout	Guinness (Ireland)	4.27	153	17.4

Harp	Harp (Ireland)	4.55	142	13
Heineken Lager	Heineken (Holland)	5	150	11.5
Heineken Light	Heineken (Holland)	3.8	99	6.8
Killian's Red	Adolph Coors	4.9	163	13.8
Michelob	Anheuser–Busch	5	155	13.3
Michelob Ultra Light	Anheuser–Busch	4.1	95	2.6
Miller High Life	Miller	4.7	143	13.1
Miller Lite	Miller	4.2	96	3.2
Molson Golden	Molson (Canada)	6.04	170	12
Molson Light	Molson (Canada)	2.41	82	9.6
Pabst Blue Ribbon	Pabst	5	153	12.01
Red Stripe Lager	Desnoes & Geddes (Jamaica)	5	153	14
Sam Adams Lager	Boston Beer	4.75	160	18
Sam Adams Light	Boston Beer	4.05	124	9.7
Schaefer	Pabst	4.6	142	12
Schlitz	Pabst	4.7	146	12.1
Yuengling Lager	D.G. Yuengling	4.4	135	12
Yuengling Light	D.G. Yuengling	3.8	98	6.6

Sources: Associated Press, writer Wayne Parry, Wednesday, June 17, 2009; www.beer100.com; www.thedailyplate.com

5 | Prohibition Years

NEW JERSEY HAS BEEN HOME TO MANY TOUGH JOBS (IRON MINERS, longshoremen), but in the fall of 1926, retired Army Colonel Ira L. Reeves took on the hardest job in our state's history—stopping New Jersey residents from drinking beer.

The Eighteenth Amendment to the Constitution, or the Liquor Prohibition Amendment, was proposed by Congress on December 18, 1917, but it took a little over a year to gather the votes needed to enact it. On January 16, 1919, three quarters of the states voted to adopt it, so the Amendment was ratified. New Jersey did not vote to adopt the Amendment but we were stuck with it. Prohibition took effect twelve months later, on January 16, 1920, prohibiting the manufacture, sale, or transportation of intoxicating liquors within the United States and its territories. It also prohibited the importation or exportation of alcoholic beverages. A new federal law known as the Volstead Act was also adopted by Congress, imposing penalties to enforce the beer ban.

The Prohibition era lasted thirteen years, and had devastating consequences to tens of thousands of people whose income was related to the sale of alcohol. New Jersey boasted fifty-one breweries before Prohibition. Only twenty-five were in business by the end of the Prohibition era in1933, and these survivors were only a fraction of their former size. In Newark alone, 2,000 jobs at breweries were eliminated. According to a New Jersey excise report in April of 1908, there were

1,925 saloons in New Jersey. All saloons, bars, and hotel lounges that sold beer and liquor were put out of business on January 16, 1920. Sure, they could convert to soda or low-alcohol beer, but there was low demand in those markets.

New Jersey was overwhelmingly a "wet" State. It was largely populated with immigrants from Italy, Germany, Ireland, and Poland who valued Old World traditions that included social drinking. Wine and beer were considered completely harmless. Even children were often permitted to drink at the dinner table. The *beer ban* seemed like a joke to these fiercely independent people. The people of New Jersey were also more progressive and sophisticated than the Bible thumping Prohibitionists of the rural Midwest states where the Eighteenth Amendment was supported. Prohibition just had no chance in Jersey, where people seem to pick and choose which laws *really* need to be followed, especially when it comes to alcohol consumption.

Union members in Newark, New Jersey protest against Prohibition, carrying signs that read, "We Want Beer," October 31, 1931.

Many local police officers, local authorities, newspapers, and even some clergy were against Prohibition. Even the New Jersey Governor was openly anti-Prohibition. Edward Edwards, elected as governor in 1919, publicly announced himself to be "as wet as the Atlantic Ocean" and he vowed to make New Jersey "wet" again. When the federal government adopted Prohibition, New Jersey was one of only three States that refused to ratify the amendment. The good governor's resistance was futile because the ban was enforced by the feds.

> *Mother's in the kitchen washing out the jugs,*
> *Sister's in the pantry bottling the suds,*
> *Father's in the cellar mixin' up the hops,*
> *Johnny's on the front porch watchin' for the cops.*
>
> Prohibition song by unknown author.

"THE PROHIBITION SAINT PATRICK OF NEW JERSEY"

Prohibition was failing miserably in New Jersey, so six years after alcohol was banned nationally, the Federal Prohibition Bureau appointed fifty-four-year-old, Col. Ira L. Reeves to run the New Jersey Prohibition Agency. Perhaps Colonel Reeves did not realize what he was getting himself into. He confidently proclaimed himself to be the "Prohibition St. Patrick of New Jersey" who would drive the bootleggers out of the state, just as St. Patrick drove the snakes out of Ireland. Reeves immediately ran into steady resistance and lack of cooperation from local authorities.

Naturally, when a law creates an artificial shortage, demand creates lucrative opportunities for illegal operations. Bootlegging (illegally making, transporting, and selling alcoholic beverages) became big business. Beer pubs had a choice: They could shut down and try to make a living selling soda; they could sell beer with 0.5 percent alcohol content (which nobody wanted); or they could sell beer illicitly at a nice profit. It was not necessary to be too secretive to run a speakeasy at the time. Local police officers (many of whom were Irish immigrants) were sympathetic to the cause. Some were bribed. Some just "looked the other way."

Newark became the bootleg capital of the United States. According to a federal crime hearing in Washington (the 1951 Kefauver Committee), 40 percent of all illegal alcohol during the Prohibition era was funneled into the United States through Newark.

It was fitting that Newark became the bootlegging capital because Reeves had located the New Jersey headquarters of the Federal Prohibition Enforcement Bureau in Newark at the corner of Broad and West Kinney streets. Despite the location of the Prohibition headquarters, Newark's illegal booze business thrived because the local police, prosecutors, and population were almost entirely sympathetic to the bootleggers.

One of Reeve's friends teased him about his lack of success, while the friend openly drank what he thought was authentic Black Horse Ale.

A can of Black Horse from a more recent vintage.

Some time later, Reeves raided a filthy New Jersey farm and found a pile of counterfeit Black Horse Ale labels and dead rats floating in the open vats of beer. Not lacking a sense humor, Reeves sent the labels and rat to his friend.

Newspaper headlines from the late 1920s reveal the wild and often humorous attempts to enforce the unpopular ban. According to newspaper stories in the late 1920s, federal Prohibition agents followed up on every reported sighting of the Jersey Devil. The agents believed that sightings of the mythical creature were linked to moonshiners in the Pine Barrens, and the agents sought to find out what the witnesses had been drinking to make them see such a thing.

It was reported that thousands of bottles, flasks, and kegs which had been seized and accumulated over the years, were finally smashed to pieces in the basement of the Mercer County Courthouse. The smell of stale beer and alcohol spread through the Trenton halls of justice for days.

A retired basketball player named Moe Katzman opened a restaurant in 1925 called the Mansion House right across the street from the courthouse in Hackensack. Katzman had played for the Boston Celtics and owned the local Flying Eagle bus line. He was well-known and well-liked throughout Bergen County so he had no problem getting the nod from local politicians and officials. Katzman claimed that he "never paid a nickel for the permission. They just did me a favor, and I was protected." One day he was arrested for serving beer to an undercover federal agent who was unaware of Katzman's local "status." He was taken across the street to the courthouse to be charged. When Judge Charles McCarthy saw him, the judge allegedly said, "Get out of here, Moe," and immediately released him. He was never hassled again.

Kegs smashed.

The public offered no assistance to federal Prohibition agents. One example comes from a federal raid in Oradell (Bergen County) About forty people were enjoying dinner and cocktails at a local hotel-restaurant that was known for fine food, illicit beer and uncut whiskey. The feds busted in, cleared the room and began to seize all of the illegal booze, but they had a hard time bringing the seized beverages back. The angry diners had slashed every one of the agents' tires.

Trenton was also openly resistant to the beer ban. Speakeasies illegally but openly operated in several spots along Chambersburg, South Broad Street, and State Street. It was reported that the police chief, William Walter, personally guaranteed the protection of bootleggers, and he threatened to arrest any federal Prohibition enforcement agent who carried a gun in Trenton. Purportedly, Chief Walter was not above taking a bribe, and his best friend, Victor Cooper, was known as the "beer baron" of Trenton.

Under this beer-friendly environment, Trenton flourished with speakeasies. Chief Walter was quoted as estimating at least 800 illegal beer pubs in Trenton. One such dive "secretly" operated on Chancery Lane—across the street from the police station.

Newspapers reported that on January 20, 1927, Col. Reeves (the federal Prohibition Czar of New Jersey) sent three of his men to raid a warehouse located at Market and Broad streets in Trenton. As soon as the agents arrived, they were met by a threatening mob of local residents who did not want their beer supply to be disrupted. As the crowd grew closer, one of the feds fired a warning shot into the air, and the gun shot was heard by a local patrolman. The cop immediately took control of the situation. He arrested the federal agents for carrying guns without licenses! The Trenton police chief, William Walter, explained, "If Col. Reeves can employ none other than gun-toting operatives, he had better keep them in Newark.... We don't want them here." It was clear that Trenton was a "wet" city despite the federal ban.

DREAM OF PROSPERITY

Last night I dreamed that the Volstead law had been amended permitting the sale of beer (Oh! what a grand and glorious feeling!). Immediately 100,000 carpenters, bricklayers and laborers went to work building and refitting breweries; 50,000 brewery truck drivers, helpers, vatmen and coppersmiths were hired; and 100,000 printers were put to work printing beer labels. Bottle works and barrel makers engaged thousands more. Bookkeepers, stenographers, clerks, and salesmen found ready employment by the hundreds of thousands. Thousands of farmers left the city and returned to farms to raise hops and barley. 150,000 musicians went to work in the beer gardens. There was no unemployment. The country hummed with industry. The tax secured from the sale of beer was placed in a fund that was used for an old age pension. Then the scene changed—I saw 1,000,000 bootleggers holding a protest meeting.

Prohibition era postcard depicting a man dreaming of "happy days" when the beer ban would be over.

MEDICINAL BEER?

Beer was commonly prescribed by doctors before Prohibition for a variety of ailments including nervousness and hysteria. The alcohol in beer obviously has a calming effect so it was thought by some to be medicinal. Shortly before retiring, U.S. Attorney General A. Mitchell Palmer issued a ruling that the federal Prohibition law (The Volstead Act) did not prevent physicians from prescribing beer and wine for "medicinal purposes." This ruling allowed doctors to prescribe beer to patients who complained of stress or anxiety. Palmer, known as the Fighting Quaker, was best known for directing controversial "Palmer Raids" on alleged anarchist and communist organizations. He served as the Attorney General from March 5, 1919, until March 4, 1921. One of Palmer's first acts was to release 10,000 aliens of German ancestry taken into custody during World War I. This, along with his ruling on "medicinal beer" made Palmer very popular among German-Americans.

Jersey residents celebrated Palmer's ruling, and breweries lined up for permits to produce medicinal beer. Most states still prohibited medicinal beer under state laws, but nine states—including New Jersey— had no state law against it. Following Palmer's new ruling, a Chicago doctor reportedly issued 7,000 prescriptions over the course of a few weeks. Colonel Jacob Rupert, of the Rupert Brewery (who later purchased the New York Yankees) was quoted in newspapers as saying: "I am happy that the authorities have recognized the therapeutic value of beer. It has been recognized for centuries by the medical profession."

Unfortunately, Palmer's ruling was only a regulatory interpretation of the Prohibition law. Federal lawmakers went right to work drafting new laws to snuff out medicinal beer. Senator Frank B. Willis of Ohio and Representative Robert S. Campbell of Kansas quickly introduced a bill that would forbid the prescription of beer and strictly limit the prescription of wine and spirits. Doctors and pharmacists argued that beer possessed therapeutic value and that Congress had no right to restrict physicians in their practice of medicine. By the summer of 1921, The Willis-Campbell Act was passed by Congress and became law throughout the country. Medicinal beer became a historical footnote. Alas, patients in "need" of a beer on a Friday evening could not get help from their doctor.

THE END OF THE BEER BAN

Eventually even Colonel Reeves caught on and he resigned from his post after just eight months as New Jersey's Prohibition czar. Although he was never a drinker, Reeves became a full convert, even making a profit from speaking out against Prohibition. He determined that Prohibition was unenforceable and was turning good citizens into law breakers. He lectured and wrote anti-Prohibition articles, and he joined an anti-Prohibition organization in Chicago known as the Crusaders. In 1931, Reeves published a book, *Ole Rum River* about his time in New Jersey. Colonel Reeves wrote: "There were just as many bootleggers, making bigger profits than before.… There were doubtless just as many wildcat stills, cutting plants, breweries, ale plants, roadhouses, saloons

President Franklin Delano Roosevelt repealing Prohibition laws.

and speakeasies as before my ambitious crusade.... I then realized what all the other administrators in the United States had learned—the Prohibition laws are unenforceable."

After thirteen years, the Prohibition "error" finally ended on March 22, 1933, with the adoption of the Twenty-first Amendment to the Constitution (repealing the Eighteenth Amendment).

The Amendment took effect at midnight on April 7, 1934. Breweries were initially allowed to brew and sell what was known as "3.2 beer"— beer with no more that 3.2 percent alcohol level. In New Jersey only the Krueger Brewery at 75 Belmont Avenue, Newark, was ready to begin selling beer right away. It sold beer by the cup right from its brewery doors. Newspapers reported that it took two days to restore order in front of the brewery. According to Will Anderson's book, *From Beer to Eternity*, more than one million barrels of beer were consumed on April 7, 1934 (that's over two million six-packs per hour!).

BEER BREAK: *HEALTH*

Two guys walk into a bar... and lower their risk of heart attack.

Several studies have concluded that beer (in moderate amounts) can be good for your health:

Heart Disease—We all know that beer is fat free, but a researcher has found that moderate beer drinkers (one to two a day at the most) have a 30–40 percent lower rate of coronary heart disease compared to those who don't drink. Beer contains a similar amount of polyphenols (antioxidants) as red wine and 4–5 times more than white wine. Beer is also rich in B vitamins which have been linked to a decreased risk of heart disease (*Texas Southwestern Medical Center*, May 1999).

Kidney Stones—A Finnish-U.S. study of beer-drinking, middle-aged men in 1999 revealed that there was a 40 percent lower risk of kidney stones in beer drinkers, but the researchers were stumped as to whether the results were due to water, alcohol, or hops (*American Journal of Epidemiology*, 1999).

Osteoporosis—Two studies suggest that moderate beer consumption may help prevent osteoporosis, a disease in which bones become fragile and more likely to break. (*Journal of Bone and Mineral Research*, February 2004; *British Journal of Nutrition*, March 2004).

Cancer—A compound found only in hops (xanthohumol) is a strong antioxidant and is hoped to be a preventative treatment against prostate and colon cancer. But there's a catch, of course, the molecule exists only in trace amounts, so a person would have to drink about 120 gallons of beer (roughly 1,300 12-ounce bottles) every day to reap the benefits.

Of course the high calorie content of beer could be problematic.

6 | New Jersey's Beer Mob

Every book about New Jersey should include a few good Mob stories, and we didn't have to look very hard to find stories involving beer and organized crime. Many early breweries were based in Newark, Jersey City, and Elizabeth so it was inevitable that Jersey's "good fellas" would get involved from time to time. During Prohibition, Jersey crime bosses made fortunes smuggling illegal beer. It was a perfect storm. People wanted beer which was banned by an unpopular federal law. Huge breweries stood idle or were converted to less profitable businesses such as producing soda. Local politicians and police typically looked the other way. Organized crime was more than happy to step in to connect supply with demand. Brewing illegal beer was highly profitable, and they would stop at nothing to protect their illicit business.

Prohibition was pushed through by well–intentioned religious conservatives. Reasonable minds may differ on the morality of the issue, but there is no doubt that Prohibition was an economic disaster and presented a boom to the underworld. Just before beer was outlawed, there were 1,150 breweries operating in the United States producing fifty million barrels of beer each year. It was a prosperous business and the brewers paid income taxes of over $150 million dollars each year. Aside from the obvious direct impact on the brewers and their employees, there were countless other industries that relied on the production of beer. Fifteen million American acres had been dedicated to growing barley, hops, and rice, which are the prime ingredients of beer. Prohibition also crushed small businesses that produced barrels, bottles, caps, labels, pumps, and pasteurizing equipment that were used by the breweries.

Sure, some of these businesses converted for the production of soda or low-alcohol beer, but most just folded due to lack of demand. The public's demand for low-alcohol near beer was just 5 percent of what the market had been for real beer. Of the 1,150 master brewers in America prior to Prohibition, 986 stopped making beer in this country. Many opened breweries in Canada or returned to Europe.

The unintended economic impact of Prohibition created a perfect storm. Supplies needed to make beer were abundant and cheap, abandoned breweries could easily be bought for next to nothing, and there was an enormous unmet demand for beer by citizens who resented the new law.

Owners and employees at bars and restaurants also suffered. Many neighborhood pubs were family-owned and the families had little opportunity to earn a living elsewhere. Many New Jersey neighborhoods were full of new immigrants from Europe who were used to drinking beer as a primary family beverage. They liked beer and felt it was harmless. They considered the government's interference as ill-conceived and insulting. They wanted their beer and were willing to buy it even if it was illegal.

Most of the men who owned and ran breweries had made their fortunes before Prohibition. They were high-standing members of their communities, and often also were public servants. These Old-World craftsmen were not enticed toward illegal trafficking of beer. The vast majority of brewery owners sold their facilities and moved on. Who would be interested in buying a beer brewery during Prohibition? Some facilities were converted for production of soda, but there wasn't a great need for more soda plants. Most breweries had very little value to anyone outside of organized crime. The Mob saw them as golden opportunities.

Local crime bosses who rose to the top of their neighborhoods through protection schemes, gambling, and prostitution, first expanded into running rum and whiskey, and then moved into beer. The rum runners already had built up a loyal distribution network of restaurants and speakeasies who bought their booze. It was a natural progression to supply illicit beer. Mobsters bought breweries that had been closed, and obtained licenses to produce low-alcohol beer. The licenses were typically issued in the name of a straw-man friend. In order to produce near beer, the brewer would have to make the real thing, and then remove the alcohol. The beer runners would simply sell some of the real beer before it underwent the process to remove the alcohol. Some went so far as to install secret underground pipes that were used to move the real beer into an adjacent building so that inspectors could never find any barrels or bottles of real beer in the brewery.

Everyone knew this was happening. Beer was readily available, but very few people in New Jersey cared to stop it.

PHILLY FEDS RAID THE RISING SUN BREWERY

The Rising Sun Brewery was secretly owned by Abner "Longy" Zwillman through front men, and it was widely known to be producing beer during the Prohibition years of the early 1930s. It was based in a red brick building in the Union Square section of Elizabeth and had been raided four times—leading to four acquittals. New Jersey was a so-called "wet state," overwhelmingly anti-Prohibition, and juries rarely convicted brewers.

Embossed bottle from
The Rising Sun Brewery.

On September 19, 1930, the U.S. Prohibition Administrator in Philadelphia sent agent John G. Finiello and five agents on a secret incursion into New Jersey to raid the Rising Sun Brewery. There was a federal Prohibition office based right in Newark, New Jersey, but apparently the Philadelphia office had some time on their hands and thought they could succeed where the Jersey agents had failed on four prior occasions. To reduce the likelihood of any leaks, the Philadelphia feds launched the raid without giving any prior notice to the local police in Elizabeth or to the federal agents based in Newark.

In spite of these efforts at secrecy, plans for the raid still leaked out. The agents reported that they were involved in what appeared to be an intentional hit-and-run before they even reached the New Jersey border. The collision eliminated one vehicle but they squeezed six agents into one car and continued their ill-fated mission to Elizabeth.

When they arrived at the brewery the feds charged in and rounded up eleven employees in the boiler room. As soon as the agents let their guard down, they were swarmed by a dozen gunmen who were waiting in the brewery's offices across Marshall Street. The gangsters quickly disarmed five of the agents, but Agent Finiello had been in different part of the brewery. When he came upon the gunmen, one of them reportedly shouted, "There's Finiello, give it to him!" He was shot to death. Having accomplished their goal, the crew took off leaving the remaining five agents and brewery employees behind.

The raid resulted in the destruction of 100,000 gallons of beer and twenty-one indictments against the low-level brewery staff, but the murder of Agent Finiello became a cold case. A few Mob-related men were named as suspects, but no arrests were made for the murder. Prosecutors believed that Finiello was specifically targeted because he had double-crossed a Mob-related brewer in South Jersey. He had accepted a $10,000 bribe to cancel plans to raid a brewery in South Jersey, but agent Finiello turned the money over to the Agency and proceeded with the raid anyway. His assassination in the Rising Sun Brewery is believed to have been payback.

Nicholas Delmore was the prime suspect. He was alleged to be a silent partner in the Rising Sun Brewery and he owned a bar in Berkeley

Heights called the Maple Grove Inn. Although he had been active in politics in Berkeley Heights, local authorities could not locate him.

Three years after the shooting, Delmore was finally arrested at his home. He was indicted and tried for murdering Agent Finiello, but was found not guilty. The prosecution's main witness was August Gobel who worked in the boiler room of the brewery and witnessed the shooting. Fortunately for Nicholas Delmore, Mr. Gobel was unable to testify. He was shot to death in the boiler room of the brewery prior to the trial.

ABNER LONGY ZWILLMAN

Although he's never been the subject of any movies, the biggest beer and whiskey runner on the East Coast was New Jersey's Abner Longy Zwillman (1904–1959). He was known as the "Al Capone of New Jersey." Zwillman made his name and fortune smuggling and selling illegal beer and whiskey, and he rose to become a member of the "Big Six" Mafia ruling commission along with Charles "Lucky" Luciano, Meyer Lansky, Frank Costello, Joe Adonis, and Ben "Bugsy" Siegel (or "Big Seven" if you include Lepke Buchalter of Murder, Inc.). He grew from being a poor fruit peddler to earning $2 million per year, and he dated the famous platinum blond movie star, Jean Harlow.

Zwillman was born in Newark and grew up in an extremely poor family with six brothers and sisters. His father was an uneducated immigrant from Russia who struggled to support his large family. They often skipped meals. At age twelve Abner began to work as a street peddler, selling fruit from a horse-drawn wagon. He was quiet, polite, and very tall at 6'2"—so people began referring to him as *der Langer* which is Yiddish for "the tall one." This nickname became "Longy" on Newark's Third Ward near Broome Street.

Although he was polite and well-liked in his neighborhood, Longy also acquired a reputation for being street-smart and willing to fight. Longy ran errands for the local political boss, Alderman Joseph Mann, who ran Newark's Third Ward. The alderman liked Longy and gave him valuable lessons on the way things worked in Newark in the early 1900s. When his father died in 1918, Longy was forced to quit school to help support his family. At just fourteen, he took up a route delivering milk to homes.

By sixteen, Zwillman expanded into running the numbers racket in his neighborhood. He already knew all of the local merchants and made deliveries to many homes, so he had a fully developed customer base. The "numbers game" or "policy" was like the lottery of the time. Customers would select three numbers and bet a nickel, dime, or quarter that their number would come in. The winning number was typically based on a derivative of each day's published stock market volume or combined bets at the local race track. Longy was better organized than others, and he quickly grew a reputation for honoring all winning bets—a trait that some other bookies did not share. He paid off shop owners to "take numbers" for him and he paid off the local patrolmen to look the other way.

Longy had grown a large numbers racket. In the same year, the Volstead Act went into effect, opening the door to an enormous financial opportunity. Zwillman wasn't formally educated but he was perceptive and understood how the marketplace worked. He understood that people wanted their beer and they did not see anything wrong with buying it illegally. He knew the Prohibition law was ill-conceived and unenforceable. He once explained, "You got to be crazy not to try and make money selling something everybody wants." He knew how to supply the demand.

The onset of Prohibition was perfect timing for Longy. He had accumulated some money, a team of loyal runners, and customers throughout Newark. He started by running Canadian whiskey to eager restaurants and speakeasies in Newark. He already had police protection in place, from his years in the numbers racket. He soon formed a partnership with a local bar owner, Joseph Reinfeld, who had connections with Seagram's Distillery in Canada, and together, they began distributing Seagram's Whiskey all along the East Coast. The IRS estimates that Zwillman imported 40 percent of all illegal booze from Canada in the 1920s. Zwillman had an advantage over other bootleggers. He distributed high quality, brand-name whiskey while others sold home-made, watered-down hooch.

With beer outlawed, Longy Zwillman was able to inexpensively acquire breweries that were closed down or struggling. Through the use of front men, Longy gained control over breweries in Elizabeth,

Newark, Harrison, and elsewhere. The breweries were permitted to produce low-alcohol beer, which is brewed as normal full-alcohol beer before the alcohol content is reduced. Longy, of course, would smuggle most of the real beer out to sell; and only convert a small amount of near beer to satisfy federal inspection agents. It was estimated that Zwillman made over $2 million per year during Prohibition.

Zwillman made friendly connections with other Mob bosses in New York and Philadelphia. He became well known and respected in the underworld circles, and he organized the Big Six Mafia Ruling Commission which controlled all gambling and bootlegging on the East Coast along with (his more famous co-commissioners) Charles Lucky Luciano, Meyer Lansky, Frank Costello, Joe Adonis, and Ben Bugsy Siegel.

Longy was supplying most of the restaurants and back-door taverns through New Jersey, so he sought to expand into the retail market as well. He approached the other members of the Big Six, and convinced them to invest with him in a string of roadside restaurants which would sell Zwillman's beer. The partnership provided another outlet for Longy's beer, but it also helped to cement his relationship with the New York Mob leaders, who supervised the gambling at the restaurants. Most speakeasies were tough places where a guy would not want to bring his wife or girlfriend. Longy and his New York partners sought to provide high-end places that would be more appealing to upper-income New Jersey residents. They focused on Hudson and Bergen County restaurants such as Costa's Barn in Lodi and the Carriage Club in Florham Park.

As he accumulated millions of dollars, Zwillman often sought to legitimize his image. For example, he offered a reward for the return of the Lindbergh baby in 1932, and he contributed to charities, including $250,000 to a Newark slum-clearing project. He helped poor families in Newark, and used his bootlegging trucks to deliver free turkeys throughout Newark's poor neighborhoods every Thanksgiving. It was estimated that he donated $10,000 worth of food every Thanksgiving and $15,000 worth of food every Christmas until the year he died. During the years of the Great Depression, Zwillman personally delivered $1,000 each week to Mount Carmel's first soup kitchen, located in the basement of Saint Patrick's Church on Mulberry Street in Newark.

Longy used his beer money to diversify into many businesses. Aside from the illegal breweries, whiskey running, and gambling businesses, he held a lot of real estate, a cigarette vending machine business in Newark, a brickyard in Staten Island, a salami factory in Brooklyn, a small steel mill, a G.M. truck dealership, a stake in a Hollywood studio, and pieces of three Las Vegas hotel casinos including the Mob-owned Flamingo Hotel and Casino which had been built by Bugsy Siegel. Zwillman owned the Hudson and Manhattan Railroad line which later became the PATH train when it was taken over by the Port Authority. His business acumen was even recognized in an article published in *The Wall Street Journal.*

Dutch Schultz, a famous New York gangster, was not happy about being shut out of the Big Six Mafia ruling commission. He repeatedly ran into territory conflicts, and drew too much attention to himself with public shootings. The final straw seems to have been Schultz's plan to rub out a New York prosecutor named Thomas Dewey. The other Mob bosses knew that a public "hit" like that would draw too much attention. It wasn't good business. They could not reason with the Dutchman so Longy Zwillman and the other members of Mob Ruling Commission agreed to take him out. They hired a hit squad known as Murder, Inc., to do the deed. Murder, Inc., was a Brooklyn gang of Jewish thugs that performed hits for other gangsters.

Dutch made a habit out of ending his day at a Newark restaurant called the Palace Chop House at 12 East Park Street, so it was decided to hit him there. Zwillman had almost complete control over the Newark police and politicians so it was the logical place. On October 23, 1935, the Dutchman and a few of his men were reviewing the day's business at the Chop House. He was shot while standing in the men's room and died a few days later.

Many Mob historians and writers consider this Newark shooting to have marked the beginning of the end for the gangsters of this era. Prohibition was over. The Dutchman was dead. Lucky Luciano was convicted and deported. Lepke Buchalter, the boss of Murder, Inc., was sentenced to death in the electric chair for unrelated charges.

Following the shooting at the Palace Chop House, Longy was questioned by the Newark police and the FBI, but he had a strong alibi and was released. The murder of Dutch Schultz in Newark increased the FBI's focus on Longy Zwillman. The director of the FBI personally requested all files on Longy and directed the agents in Newark to focus on building a tax evasion case against him—as they had used to take down Al Capone in Chicago. This new focus eventually led to a trial of Longy Zwillman for tax evasion in 1956. He avoided conviction, but one of his henchmen was indicted in 1959 for bribing members of the jury. Longy hung himself in the basement of his West Orange mansion on February 26, 1959.

MAX HASSEL—JERSEY'S GENTLEMAN BEER BARON

Most beer barons of the Prohibition era started as street hustlers and criminals before starting to smuggle beer. Max Hassel took an unusual route to becoming a big-time beer bootlegger. Guys like Longy Zwillman, Waxey Gordon, Lucky Luciano, and Meyer Lansky spent their early years running gambling rings, prostitution, and protection rackets. Max Hassel was different. He came from a law-abiding family that settled in Reading, Pennsylvania, from Latvia (which was part of Russia at the time). Max was born Mendel Gasel on April 24, 1900. When he came to America as a young boy, he Americanized his name to Max Hassel and his father soon began using the Hassel name as well.

Max's father ran a small business as a tailor, and Max had a typical childhood. He quit school at fourteen, which was not uncommon in immigrant families in 1914, and he started a variety of small businesses. He worked at a department store off and on, while he ran a paper route, and he hired friends to make hand-rolled cigars. He also had a door-to-door sales route for household products. As his businesses thrived, he hired more people to cover his paper and sales routes, and he rented stores to sell his cigars. His cigar business took off. The cigars that he made were considered to be of the highest quality and his stores were crowded with business men who often spoke of the on-coming Prohibition laws.

By nineteen, Max was already an experienced business man. He supervised an organized team of delivery and salespeople, and he had contacts for funding his ventures. When Prohibition was adopted, most legitimate beer producers soon exited the business and offered their breweries for sale. The closed breweries were of little value for any legitimate use, because there was very low demand for near beer. At twenty-two, Max bought his first brewery in Reading using a straw man to hold title. Profits were staggering. It typically cost about $5 to produce a keg of beer which then could be wholesaled to a bootlegger for $16 to $20, or could be sold directly to a speakeasy or restaurant for $22 to $32. A brewery that could produce 100,000 kegs per year could generate a profit of $1 million tax free. Over the next few years Max acquired or leased a few other breweries in and around Reading, Pennsylvania, using friends and associates to hold the leases and deeds.

Unlike New Jersey, the governor of Pennsylvania was a strict Prohibitionist, so Pennsylvania soon began to crack down on breweries. Hassel made millions while playing cat and mouse with inspectors. He bribed officials and kept distributing his beer as quickly as he could brew it. Like his cigars, Max grew a reputation for selling the finest quality beer. The IRS estimated his income to be over $1 million per year in 1924 and 1925. Eventually the feds caught up with him and by the end of 1925, all of his breweries were shut down. Max was tried for tax evasion but avoided jail time. He paid back-taxes of $150,000 and shifted his attention to New Jersey where the climate was much friendlier to illicit beer.

Max acquired the Camden County Cereal Beverage Company in 1928. In a brilliant move, he hired a former federal Prohibition agent, Yates Fetterman, to open the Jersey territory. Fetterman knew all of the speakeasies and illicit distributors, so he quickly made deals to flood the area with Hassel's beer. Prohibition agents were paid salaries of just $2,000 to $3,000 per year, so it was not hard to influence them with the stream of money generated through the illegal beer trade.

Max was different from the other Jersey beer smugglers. He never carried a gun and didn't use typical Jersey strong-arm tactics. He even forbid his bodyguards from carrying guns. By all accounts, he was just an honest gentleman conducting an illegal business in a world of violent gangsters. He believed that his reputation and business savvy could lead him to success, and keep him out of harm's way. Mickey "the Muscle" would change all of that.

Mickey the Muscle Duffy was a strong-arm thug who operated out of Philly and Camden, and he noticed the fast success that Max was enjoying in Camden. He visited Max and offered to buy into the Camden Brewery but Max rejected him. Perhaps Max didn't realize that the Muscle's offer was not to be refused. One night when Max was working in the office of the Camden brewery, Duffy and his goons paid him a visit. They simply carried Max out and literally dumped him in the street, informing him that the brewery now belonged to Duffy.

Max, being practical, waited a few weeks and negotiated a partnership. Max didn't want a war, and Mickey needed Max's business acumen and contacts, so they teamed up. Knowing that Mickey the Muscle was living a high-risk, violent life style, Max made a good choice. Mickey Duffy was dead within two years, so Max regained full control of the brewery.

By 1929, Max began to expand north through New Jersey via a syndicate he formed with Waxey Gordon and Max Greenberg. He leased a penthouse suite in Elizabeth's new Carteret Hotel. He didn't try to force anyone out and he was careful not to impose on anyone's territory. He started by just making investments in a few breweries and he gradually took controlling positions. Along with his partners, Waxey Gordon and Max Greenberg, "the Jersey Trio" took control of the Eureka Brewery in Paterson; the Union City Brewery; the Peter Hauck Brewery and Harrison Brewery in Harrison; the Rising Sun Brewery and Peter Heide Brewery in Elizabeth; the Hygeia Brewery in Passaic; the Hensler Brewery in Newark; and the Orange Brewery. They controlled the breweries through straw men and phantom companies, so it is impossible to know how many facilities they ultimately controlled. Federal agents believed that the trio controlled a total of sixteen breweries in New York and Pennsylvania by 1933.

Orange Brewery bottle.

Embossed Hensler bottle.

A bottle from the
Rising Sun Brewery.

Hygeia Brewing
Company of Passaic.

As the Jersey Trio cornered the Jersey beer market and made millions, they started to gain more attention and run into problems. New York gangster Dutch Schultz ran a string of speakeasies in the Bronx and often purchased beer from Max and his partners. The Dutchman knew a good thing when he saw it so he wanted in. The trio declined his offer, so Schultz responded by unleashing his thugs to highjack Jersey beer trucks and redirect them to his New York clubs. Schultz was known to be violent and unpredictable, so Max and his partners did their best to stay out of his way and avoid a war.

They also were getting some heat from Meyer Lansky, Frank Costello, and Bugsy Siegel. As Prohibition was coming to its inevitable end, the Big Six crime bosses sought to control the market. We will never know for sure who planned it, but it is clear that members of the Mob's ruling party wanted to take down this powerful trio of Jersey beer smugglers.

Max Hassel must have felt the heat. After refusing to carry a weapon throughout his life, he changed course. He began to carry a gun, and allowed his bodyguards to carry guns, too. He expanded his suite to encompass the entire eighth floor of the Carteret, and he rarely left his suite.

The *New York Times* reported that Max Greenberg and Max Hassel were shot in the head multiple times on April 12, 1933, in Hassel's suite. Both men were found with pistols and carrying permits issued by the Asbury Park Police Chief. Although the police questioned many potential witnesses, including the victims' bodyguards, hotel staff and guests, no one witnessed the shootings. No one saw anyone coming or going. No one heard anything. In short, no one would talk.

Although there were no witnesses, the Union County Prosecutor's office indicted Frankie Carbo—a known hit man for Murder, Inc. Carbo had been arrested for murder on five previous occasions, but was never convicted. In all of the prior cases against Carbo, either there were no witnesses or the witness was shot before trial. In this case, no witnesses would come forward so the charges were dismissed before trial.

Some speculate that the double hit was ordered by Longy Zwillman who secretly took control over the Harrison Beverage Company two weeks after the murders. According to Mark Stuart's book, *Gangster #2: Longy Zwillman*, the murders were ordered by Longy as part of a beer turf war. There are several possibilities. Maybe Dutch Schultz organized the hit, or perhaps it was Meyer Lansky and his Group of Six.

Investigators found documents in the dead men's safe that revealed organized crime's involvement with breweries. Among the treasure of documents that the feds found in Max's suite, there was a list of thirty federal agents. Next to twenty of the names was written "OK." Next to ten of the names was written "Do Not Deal."

Immediately following the double murder, federal Prohibition agents began to investigate organized crime's secret links to breweries that were licensed to produce low-alcohol beer. Court orders were issued on April 18, 1933, seeking to shut down five breweries for false statements as to ownership interests in their permit applications. The feds sought to shut down the Harrison Beverage Company (which was secretly owned by the gunned-down racketeers, Max Greenberg and Max Hassel), Eureka Cereal Beverage Company in Paterson, Superior Manufacturing Company of Newark, the Camden County Beverage Company, and the Union City Brewing Company. During federal hearings, former heavyweight boxing champ Jack Dempsey was alleged to be a front man for Max Greenberg's secret ownership of the Harrison Brewery. Dempsey denied any involvement.

The timing of this shooting was very fortunate for the legitimate beer industry and society as a whole. Prohibition had just come to an end on March 22, 1933. Had it not been for these murders and the investigation that followed, New Jersey's organized crime bosses would have been in prime position to take over the legitimate beer business.

Within hours of the shooting, the trio's breweries in Newark, Elizabeth, Paterson, and Union City were cleaned out. All vats were drained dry and all kegs were shipped out. We will never know whether it was the work of the New York Mob taking the spoils of their victory, or possibly Waxey Gordon purging the breweries of all evidence before the federal investigators came calling. Waxey was the sole remaining partner, but he didn't escape punishment. Waxey Gordon was indicted two weeks later on April 27, 1933, and spent ten years in jail.

WAXEY GORDON—THE JERSEY TRIO'S ENFORCER

Irving Wexler, also known as "Waxey" Gordon, started out picking pockets in the streets of Philadelphia. The name Waxey was derived from his last name and his "waxey smooth" pick-pocketing skills. (Some historians attribute the name to his smooth skin.) He grew to be a collector and enforcer for local bookies and, in 1920, he naturally progressed into bootlegging during Prohibition.

With financial backing from Arnold Rothstein (who orchestrated the Black Sox Scandal in which the 1919 World Series was fixed), Waxey expanded into northern New Jersey running whiskey. He had a small fleet of ships that he used to smuggle high-end brand-name whiskey from Canada into Jersey for distribution throughout the East Coast.

Things were going great and he was making millions—until 1925. The wife of one of his ship captains got mad at her husband and spilled the beans. The ship captain was questioned and Waxey was arrested for bootlegging. The ship captain knew too much about the size and scope of Waxey's operation, so Waxey was facing a certain conviction plus potential charges for tax evasion. Before the matter could reach trial, the captain was found shot to death. After a short investigation, it was ruled a suicide and Waxey walked free of all charges due to a lack of witnesses.

Flush with cash, Waxey bought the Sprattler and Mennel's Brewery in Paterson so that he could create the appearance of a legitimate business selling legal near beer while really brewing and distributing illegal full-alcohol beer. He paid next to nothing for the brewery because it had no value as a legitimate business.

He already had built up a distribution network from his whiskey business, and he had been paying off all of the right people. All he needed was to make nice with the local crime boss in the area. He reached out to Longy Zwillman and got his blessings. In fact, Longy is credited with teaching Waxey to run fire hoses along the city's existing underground sewer lines so that his illegal beer could be pumped directly out of the brewery and into a warehouse across town. When federal agents would come calling at the brewery, they would only find the legal low-alcohol beer.

Waxey became a partner and provided the muscle for the Jersey Trio and business was good for a few years. Everything came crashing down for Waxey Gordon in 1930. Like Al Capone, he was brought down by some accountants with sharp pencils. Waxey had run into a bitter turf war with Dutch Schultz and Meyer Lansky. Waxey accused Lansky of highjacking one of his shipments of illegal booze. The dispute grew more and more heated, so Lansky's childhood buddy, Lucky Luciano had his brother, Tony, leak incriminating documents about Waxey's financial holdings to IRS agents in Philadelphia. The IRS alleged that Waxey had made $1.34 million from beer alone in 1930.

Two weeks after his partners, Max Hassel and Max Greenberg, were gunned down in Elizabeth, Waxey Gordon was indicted. He claimed that he was a lowly salesperson just working for the slain beer barons, but the jury didn't buy it. On December 1, 1933, he was found guilty and sentenced to ten years. Four days later, on December 5, Prohibition was repealed. On the same day, Waxey's nineteen-year-old son was killed in a car crash on his way home from medical school in North Carolina.

Waxey was released in 1940, but was convicted again in 1951 and sentenced to Alcatraz where he died in 1952.

BEER WAR OF NEWARK: LONGY VS. THE BOOT

As told in Mark Stuart's outstanding book on Longy Zwillman, New Jersey's least famous gangster won a deadly war over who would supply Newark's restaurants and speakeasies with illegal beer and whiskey.

As detailed above, Zwillman was New Jersey's leading supplier of beer during Prohibition. Ruggiero "Richie the Boot" Boiardo came up in the streets of Newark at about the same time as Longy Zwillman, but he did not share Longy's business sense, so his territory was limited to Newark's Little Italy—the First Ward (Seventh Avenue neighborhood bound by Route 280 to the south, Clifton Avenue to the west, Bloomfield Avenue to the north, and Broadway and Broad Street to the east).

Richie the Boot's early years were similar to Longy's. He had a milk home-delivery route as a boy, and he used the route to begin running a numbers game in his neighborhood. He would lend money and take bets as he delivered milk to homes along his route. When the Eighteenth Amendment was adopted, he made the natural progression to supplying beer to restaurants, taverns, and even homes along his route. He made and received dozens of calls each day at a public phone booth in his neighborhood, and so he earned the nickname, "Richie the Booth"— which due to North Jersey accents, morphed into "Richie the Boot."

Flush with success, Richie decided to expand his territory throughout Newark into Longy Zwillman's turf. He tried to strong-arm Longy's customers, he shot up a bar that resisted, and he murdered one of Longy's beer deliverymen. While Longy respected Richie and had stayed out of his First Ward neighborhood, he wasn't about to give up any of his turf.

One spring day, as Richie the Boot was crossing Broad Street in downtown Newark near Market Street, he was approached by three of Longy's goons. Without warning, they emptied their guns, hitting Richie eight times. He was brought to St. Michaels Hospital and lived.

Longy Zwillman had been around long enough to know that the war wasn't over, so he had his men hunt down Richie's henchmen before they could strike back. Longy's enforcers caught three of Richie's boys in a restaurant on Bloomfield Avenue. They were brought to a dark lot behind Ballantine Brewery and bashed across their knees with bats—crushing their bones and crippling the men for life.

Richie the Boot Boiardo wasn't a quitter. He set up a few of his guys in an apartment across from the Riviera Hotel where Zwillman stayed, but they never got a shot at him. Longy was too careful.

One day two women visited the front desk of the Riviera and asked to see Longy Zwillman. The desk clerk called Longy's room but tipped him off that there was something odd about these women. Longy approved the visitors and they were sent up the elevator to Zwillman's third floor suite. As the two visitors reached Longy's floor and the elevator door slid open, they were met by two bodyguards with pistols drawn.

The ladies were shaking as they were searched. The bodyguards made two interesting discoveries. The visitors had guns hidden in their dresses… and they were boys. The eighteen-year-old boys shook, prayed, and cried as Longy questioned them. One reportedly urinated in his dress. Zwillman, ever the opportunist, released the young gunmen unharmed and sent them back to Richie the Boot with a message to call him to discuss a truce.

The two bootleggers met. Each kept his original territory, and agreed to avoid any future conflicts. (Some say that Al Capone visited from Chicago to help settle the dispute.) So ended the Newark Beer War.

ATLANTIC CITY—WHERE ORGANIZED CRIME GOT ORGANIZED

The 1928 presidential election went heavily in favor of Republican Herbert Hoover, who was a staunch defender of Prohibition. It was clear that America would stay "dry," and beer smugglers would keep making millions, for at least four more years.

Organized crime really wasn't all that organized. Bootleggers were always stepping on each other's toes and getting into costly turf wars which were both bad for business, and deadly. The police, politicians, and the public were quietly in favor of the illegal beer market, but they had little patience for shootouts and mysterious disappearances. It was in everyone's best interest for beer makers to organize—setting rules and territories, and enforcing them uniformly across the nation. Where could a meeting be held to discuss such a nation-wide syndicate of bootleggers? Where else? New Jersey—Atlantic City to be specific. And who would dream up and organize such a meeting? Newark's own Abner Longy Zwillman.

After settling a vicious turf war with Richie the Boot Boiardo of Newark, Zwillman saw the value in organizing all of the big-time bootleggers across the country. He shared his idea with New York bosses Meyer Lansky and Lucky Luciano, and a meeting was set for May 14, 1929. It was the first large-scale meeting of Mob bosses. Gangsters from the eastern half of the country attended including Al Capone from Chicago, Charlie Lucky Luciano, Frank Costello, Louis Lepke Buchalter (of Murder, Inc.), Joe Adonis (of Brooklyn), Ben Siegel, Dutch Schultz of New York, Waxey Gordon of Philadelphia, and many others from the Midwest to the East Coast. Longy Zwillman was the New Jersey representative. The convention lasted for three days at the Ritz where

Lansky was honeymooning. Of course they enjoyed the finest Canadian whiskey, beer, and champagne from Longy's operation.

The group accepted Longy Zwillman's plan. A federation was formed with regional groupings. The new syndicate would control all bootlegging and gambling in each region. They agreed to fix prices for the supplies that they needed, so they would no longer bid against each other, driving costs up, and they agreed that the regional bosses would organize small territories within their region. The Eastern Region was controlled by the Group of Six. The 1929 "meeting of bosses" in Atlantic City set the stage for smooth profits until Prohibition ended in 1933.

BEER BREAK: *MORE BEER QUOTES*

"I would kill everyone in this room for a drop of sweet beer."
                                        –Homer Simpson

"Make sure that the beer—four pints a week—goes to the troops under fire before any of the parties in the rear get a drop."
                        –Winston Churchill to his Secretary of War, 1944

"I'm going to buy a boat, do a little traveling, and I'm going to be drinking beer!"
                                –John Welsh, Brooklyn bus driver
                        who won $30 million in the New York lottery

"24 hours in a day, 24 beers in a case. Coincidence?"
                                        –Stephen Wright, comedian

"I would give all my fame for a pot of ale and safety."
                                –William Shakespeare, *Henry V*

"Well ya see, Norm, it's like this. A herd of buffalo can only move as fast as the slowest buffalo. And when the herd is hunted, it is the slowest and weakest ones at the back that are killed first. This natural selection is good for the herd as a whole, because the general speed and health of the whole group keeps improving by the regular killing of the weakest members. In much the same way, the human brain can only operate as fast as the slowest brain cells. Excessive intake of alcohol, as we know, kills brain cells. But naturally, it attacks the slowest and weakest brain cells first. In this way, regular consumption of beer eliminates the weaker brain cells, making the brain a faster and more efficient machine. That's why you always feel smarter after a few beers."
                                –Cliff Clavin of *Cheers*,
                        explaining the Buffalo Theory to his buddy Norm

7 | The Beer Can: A Jersey First

THE SOUND OF OPENING A CAN OF BEER IS UNIVERSALLY RECOGNIZED among beer lovers, but very few people know that a New Jersey brewer was the first to sell beer in cans. Today, about 90 percent of beer is sold in cans and bottles, but prior to 1930 there were no beer cans and it was rare to find anyone drinking from a bottle. Beer was typically sold in kegs and it was consumed on the premises. If a patron wanted to take some beer home, some bars would sell a "to go" container of beer that was similar to a cardboard Chinese food container. Bottles were available but not widely used.

Cans were widely used at the time for storage and sale of food, but the cans could not be used for beer. Beer posed two problems to the canners. Cans could not withstand the pressure of a carbonized beverage such as beer. Remember when beer and soda cans had seams? Believe it or not, beer cans must withstand pressure over 80 pounds per square inch (psi). A normal can of corn only withstands about 30 psi before the can bursts along its seam. The other problem with canning beer was that the beer reacted badly with the tin can itself.

As the Prohibition era staggered to an end in the early 1930s, the American Can Company began experimenting with new production techniques to develop cans that could deal with "beer pressure." They strengthened the seam and developed a coating for the inside of the can that would prevent the beer from reacting with the can itself.

The Gottfried Krueger Brewing Company of Newark became the first brewer to sell beer in cans in 1935. The Krueger brewery had been a popular Jersey brewer since 1865, but thirteen years of Prohibition, a strike, and the death of its founder, Gottfried Krueger, had taken a toll on the business. The American Can Company was looking for a reputable brewer to test-market its new cans, so they made an offer that Krueger could not refuse. American Can offered to install the new canning equipment free, and Krueger would only have to pay for it if the "beer can experiment" succeeded.

Krueger needed some publicity buzz, and the brewer had nothing to lose. The canning equipment was installed in Newark and Krueger produced a test run of 2,000 cans in 1933. Krueger, however, was hesitant to proceed. It feared that it would harm its reputation if the cans exploded, or if the beer was tainted from reacting with the can material, so the first run was made available only to regular Krueger drinkers who were then polled for satisfaction. Ninety-one percent of the faithful Krueger drinkers approved of the cans.

The Krueger can with the K-man.

On January 24, 1935 the first cans of beer went on sale to the general public. Ever cautious, Krueger chose to only release the cans for sale in the small market of Richmond, Virginia. Only after the cans continued to sell well, and no one was blown up by a defective can, did Krueger rolled out mass distribution.

Krueger brochure announcing new beer cans.

American Can's efforts paid off. By the summer of 1935, it convinced Pabst to try cans. Pabst was also hesitant and it would not initially sell its top-selling Blue Ribbon in cans. Instead, it experimented by canning its export brand. By the end of 1935, thirty-seven breweries in the United States sold canned beer.

Brewers tried some unusual and creative ways to introduce this new technology to the public. Some brewers reassured the public by printing phrases such as "12 oz Same as bottle" directly on the front of the can to assure buyers that they were not being shortchanged.

One canning company, Continental Can, went so far as to develop cans that were shaped like a bottle. This can, called a cone-top, was

The innovative Krueger cans were heavily advertised to gain public acceptance.

Cone-top cans are relatively rare and valuable to collectors.

capped with a bottle cap and could be filled on the bottling lines already in place at the breweries. By contrast, brewers had to install new equipment to handle the new flat top cans.

From the beer drinker's point of view, the cone-tops opened in the same manner as the traditional bottle.

Those of us over thirty-five recall soda and beer cans that required a can opener. The "flip top" or "pull tab" cans of today were not in wide use until the 1970s. The original flat top cans required a can opener to punch a pair of holes in the top of the can. Brewers would give the can openers away with the purchase of a number of cans. The openers were often referred to as a "church key" and they were typically printed with advertising beer slogans.

Of course, when a new technology gains popularity, there is usually another industry that loses. Glass bottle companies were not willing to lose their market share without a fight. They publicly argued that beer tasted better from a bottle—the cans had the potential to add a "tinny" taste. They also implied that people should not drink what they could not see. The bottles allowed the drinker to inspect the clarity and purity of the beer. These were valid arguments, but the bottlers were at a disadvantage. They wanted to keep selling bottles to brewers but the brewers liked cans. Any public criticism of canned beer was made at the risk of alienating the brewers who the bottlers were trying to woo.

Quart bottles were popular before Prohibition, so some breweries tried out quart cans when cans became popular after Prohibition. The quart cans are especially desirable among collectors because they are so strikingly different from today's beer can.

Beer cans became temporarily rare during World War II because metals were directed toward the war effort, forcing brewers to package their beer almost entirely in bottles. The exception to this was beer packaged especially for the overseas troops.

Cans have now become the most popular beer container because of convenience. Brewers and distributors favored cans because they were (and still are) lighter and more compact to transport, and cans could be filled with beer quicker than bottles. Cans are less likely to break than bottles and they are more convenient for consumers—although some still insist that bottled beer tastes better.

BEER CAPS

The first bottle cap was invented in 1891 by William Painter of Baltimore, Maryland. He called it the "crown cork" and it became known as the "crown cap" or "crown." He made it from a sheet of steel with a thin cork disc where the cap contacts the bottle. A bottle cap opener was needed to pop it off the bottle and it could not be resealed In 1892, Painter patented the bottle cap design (U.S. patent number 468,258), and started the Bottle Seal Company, which is now known as Crown Holdings. Dan Rylands of Barnsley in the United Kingdom patented the screw cap on August 10, 1889.

In spite of these inventions, beer bottles generally had a wire-attached mechanical cap until 1915. Grolsch beer is still sold with a form of wire cap.

An increase in glass bottle production during the early twentieth century increased the demand and usage of bottle caps. By the 1930s, most beer and soft drink bottles had bottle caps.

Lyon & Sons Brewing
wire cap bottle.

Greenville Brewing
wire cap bottle.

BEER BREAK: *KEG, CAN, OR BOTTLE*

Ever notice that beer tastes best from a tap in a bar with friends?
It may not be just the surroundings. The way beer is stored and
transported has a major effect on how it tastes.

Keg Beer

Given the option, most regular beer drinkers would choose draft
beer. Keg beer retains most of the flavor that it had when it was
brewed, and it is less affected by the packaging process than canned
or bottled beer. Keg beer usually is not pasteurized so more of
the original flavor is retained. Unlike canned or bottled beer, the
taste of keg beer is not affected by the heat process involved in

pasteurization or by the filtering out of aromatic ingredients. Another key advantage is that keg beer is not affected by light and (unlike bottles and cans) kegs are typically kept refrigerated from the brewery to the tap.

Bottled Beer

Most mass-produced bottled beers have undergone rapid heat treatment or *pasteurization*. Even though it has been pasteurized, bottled beer has a limited shelf life of three to six months because it is not kept refrigerated and may be subjected to sunlight or fluorescent light. Beer keeps longer in brown bottles than in green or clear bottles. Stale beer gains a *skunky* flavor, but it is not harmful.

Canned Beer

Canned beer is typically filtered before it's canned and then pasteurized in the can, with heat. Cans eliminate the threat of light, and the insides of beer cans are treated with a nonreactive coating so the beer will not be tainted with a metallic taste. Drinking directly from a can, however, may affect the flavor because the mouth makes contact with the can. The taste of both canned and bottled beers is normally improved by pouring the beer into a glass, so the aroma of hops and other ingredients can be released.

8 | Types of Jersey Beer

ACCORDING TO THE GERMAN *REINHEITSGEBOT* BEER PURITY LAW adopted in 1516 and made famous by the recent Becks commercials, beer should be made of just three ingredients:

- Water
- Barley Malt
- Hops

Assorted roasts of barley

Brewing vats.

The original German *Reinheitsgebot* beer purity law did not even
mention yeast—which had not yet been discovered. Yeast was naturally
present in the barrels that were used.

Of course, this law isn't applicable in New Jersey or anywhere other
than Germany, but it makes the point that beer is brewed from a simple
formula. The many different brands, styles, and flavors are essentially
based on three variables, the type of grain (barley, wheat, corn, etc.), the
type of hops, and the type of yeast.

Beer is simply brewed by mashing (temperature-controlled steeping
in water) the grain—traditionally barley—to release sugar from the
grain, and then fermenting the mash with yeast. This process turns the
grain into a sugary liquid called a "wort." Once mashing is completed,
the spent grain husks are strained away from the wort.

Barley mash vat at Cricket Hill Brewery in Fairfield, New Jersey.

The wort.

Close-up of barley mash.

Yeast is then added to the wort to ferment the sugar. Fermentation produces alcohol, heat, carbon dioxide, esters, and a few trace compounds. Different varieties of yeast produce varying esters that add fruity aromas and flavors such as citrus or banana.

Postcard of Anheuser-Busch fermentation vats in Newark, circa 1951.

Hops are small flowers that are added to beer for flavor and acidity. They add the bitterness. Without hops, beer would be sweet like soda. The IBU (International Bittering Unit) is a measure of a beer's bitterness. Budweiser has a mild 11.5 IBU, Heineken weighs in at 18, and Pilsner Urquell tips the scale at 43.

Brewing beer is very simple, but brew masters distinguish the taste of their beer by varying the measurements of the ingredients; by selecting different types of grain, yeast, and hops; and by the artistry of their techniques. Some brands are known for using unusual grain such as Corona (corn) and Blue Moon (wheat). Many brewers use a proprietary yeast to create a distinctive flavor.

Beer can be broken into two major styles: lager and ale. Jersey brewers have proven that all of the many variations can be successfully produced here.

Lager beer is the world's most popular style. It originated in Germany and was brought to the U.S. by German immigrants. It is unclear who was the first to brew lager in America. Lager beer is fermented at cooler temperatures (just above freezing) and bottom-fermenting yeast is used. The cooler temperature slows down the fermentation process and yields clear, crisper, cleaner-tasting beer. Lagers are dominated by the larger international breweries, and are less flavorful than ale. Although lagers are known for their clarity and crispness, they are not necessarily light in color.

Lager can be broken down into four basic styles: American lager/pilsner, European pilsner, light beer, and dark lager. American (pale) lager is typically more carbonated, and is light in color, body, and flavor (for example, Bud, Coors, and Miller). It is similar to, and derived from, European pilsner beer, but not quite as "hoppy" as true European pilsners such as Heineken and Becks. Pilsner is a style of lager that originated in 1842 in Pilsen, Bohemia (the Czech Republic today). It was the first beer brewed with a light color. Characteristics of pilsner include a pale body, and crisp, dry finish—sometimes bitter. American lager is the most popular style in America, dominated by the mega-brands such as Coors and Budweiser.

Light lager beer is made with less hops and grain, which reduces the calories, alcohol level, and the flavor of the beer. Dark lagers are made with roasted grain (typically barley), which imparts a darker color and richer full-bodied flavor.

Examples of lagers

Style	Examples of Brands
Pilsner /American Lager	Bud, Coors, Miller,
European Pilsner	Heineken, Becks
Light Lager	Bud Light, Coors Light, Miller Lite
Dark (Dunkel) Lager	Climax Doppel Bock, Heineken Dark, Becks Dark

Ales are fermented at warmer temperatures (65 degrees) with top-fermenting yeast. The yeast works quicker to turn the sugars into alcohol and it makes for a more full-flavored, cloudy beer. The yeast bubbles at the top of the wort and creates a thick layer of floating foam. The bubbling yeast converts the sugar (from the grain) into ethyl alcohol and carbon dioxide which carbonates the beer. The yeast also creates esters (organic compounds) which impart a fruity or nutty flavor to the ale. For example, pale ales often have a citrus-like taste. Ales typically have a higher alcohol content than lagers, and a stronger, more complex flavor.

Lagers are typically served ice-cold, but ales are best served at about 50 degrees. Colder temperatures will numb the palate and some of the complex flavors will be hidden. Ales are often unfiltered or bottle-conditioned which results in a cloudier appearance. Mass produced ales are typically filtered so they are clearer with no sediment on the bottom of the bottle. The cloudiness or sediment is just harmless yeast which adds flavor. Belgian style ales are known for being bottle-conditioned. Many people are thrown-off by the cloudiness and sediment in this style of ale. Some try to gently pour the bottle without disturbing the sediment, while others will swirl the bottle to loosen the flavorful sediment. It is a matter of taste.

Ballantine was the most popular ale in America in the early 1900s, but today the more common ales are Bass, Guinness Stout, Smithwick's Irish Ale, and the Samuel Adams line of ales. Variations of ale include: honey brown ale, porter, India pale ale (IPA), and stout. Porters are darker and more full bodied. Porters usually have a more noticeable barley flavor (which can be similar to chocolate), along with a mild hop flavor. Stouts are the darkest type of beer, almost black in color. They are heavy and taste strongly of the barley.

There are countless varieties of ale including those in the table below.

Varieties of ale.

Style	Examples of Brands
Pale ale	Anchor, Sam Adams
India pale ale	Cricket Hill, Climax IPA, Sierra Nevada
Stout	Guinness
Porter	Sam Adams, Yuengling
Wheat beer	High Point, Climax, Blue Moon, Belgian White Ale
Lambic	Sam Adams Cranberry Lambic
Brown ale	Climax Nut Brown, Dundees' Honey Brown
Barley wine	Sierra Nevada Bigfoot
Cream ale	Climax Cream Ale, Genesee Cream Ale

Specialty or hybrid beers are the misfits. They include nontraditional ingredients such as pumpkin, apple, smoked barley, or nontraditional brewing procedures such as "steam ale" or "ice lager." Specialty beers such as this can be either ale or lager, depending on whether top-fermenting yeast is used.

Small beer isn't popular any more, but it was very popular when families made their own home brew. It is made from the second and third runnings from the brewer's mash—like reusing the same coffee grounds to make coffee. The first batch created the so-called "large beer" and the subsequent batches created a weaker brew with less alcohol (about 2.5 percent alcohol) and less flavor. Back when water supplies were unsafe, small beer would commonly be served to servants and even children.

It can be a bit overwhelming to scan the enormous choices available in a large market, but it is worth the effort and expense to try a few different styles and brands. There are good qualities in all of the types of beer, and sampling is fun.

BEER BREAK: *TRIVIA*

- Beer is the second most popular beverage in the world, behind tea.

- Pabst Beer is now called Pabst Blue Ribbon beer because it was the first beer to win a blue ribbon at the Chicago World's Fair in 1893.

- Monks brewing beer in the Middle Ages were allowed to drink five quarts of beer a day.

- The oldest known written recipe is for beer.

- The Pilgrims landed at Plymouth Rock because of beer. They had planned to sail further south to a warm climate, but were running low on critical supplies, including beer.

- Anheuser-Busch is the largest brewery in the U.S. It is now owned by AB-InBev of Belgium.

- Molson, Inc., is the oldest brewery in North America.

- Franklin Delano Roosevelt (FDR) was elected in 1932 because of his promise to end Prohibition.

- Samuel Adams Triple Bock is the strongest beer in the world with 17 percent alcohol by volume.

- Actors: Sandra Bullock, Bruce Willis, Tom Arnold, Chevy Chase, Kris Kristofferson, and Bill Cosby all started out as bartenders.

- Beer is a source of B-complex vitamins.

- A labeorphilist is one who collects beer bottles.

- The "33" on a bottle of Rolling Rock was originally a printer's error. It refers to the 33 words in the original slogan. It has generated enough mystery over the years that the company left it in the label.

- The beer industry contributes nearly $200 billion to U.S. economy each year.

9 | Resurgence of Jersey Brewers: Microbreweries

ABOUT 100 YEARS AGO, NEW JERSEY HAD ITS SHARE OF THE LARGEST AND most respected breweries in the country. With Pabst, Rheingold, Kruegers, and Ballantine, Jersey brewing was the seventh-largest industry in the state generating $20 million a year by 1910. Ballantine was the number-one ale in the country.

Jersey brewers went through a dark period that began with Prohibition in 1920. Almost all of New Jersey's legitimate brew masters left the business. Most of the mobsters who ran the business during Prohibition ran into legal trouble for unpaid income taxes. The Jersey breweries that survived could not compete with large national breweries like Anheuser-Busch, Coors, and Miller. Although we still offer favorable infrastructure, ports, and a beer-loving population, New Jersey has lost all of its larger breweries. Ballantine closed shop in the 1960s. The Rheingold Brewery in Orange closed its doors in 1977, followed by Pabst in Newark in 1985, leaving Anheuser-Busch as the only large brewery in New Jersey.

Anheuser-Busch, based in St. Louis, Missouri, purchased about fifty acres in Newark in the mid-1940s, and opened a brand new high-tech brewing facility there in 1951. Today, more Bud is made in New Jersey than anywhere else. The name "Budweiser" has been hotly litigated in recent years. An old brewery named "Budejovicky Budvar" in the Budweis area of the Czech Republic (formerly Pilsen, Bohemia) has

Bud can.

been selling a "Budweiser" lager for years. So far, the Czech brewery has retained the right to use the name Budweiser in Europe.

The beer story in New Jersey today is craft-brewing. Local microbrewers and brew pubs produce smaller batches of distinctive artisan beers that fill a niche ignored by the mega-breweries. Microbreweries can sell up to 15,000 barrels per year. Most sales are through distributors to local stores, restaurants, and pubs, but a few microbreweries distribute in other states. The breweries are open to the public but over-the-counter sales are limited to just two six-packs per customer.

Brew pubs are affiliated with a restaurant and are limited to selling their beer on site to retail customers. Under New Jersey law, brewpubs cannot distribute their beer through a wholesaler.

Microbreweries and brew pubs typically brew a number of specialty and seasonal brews that are more full-bodied and flavorful than the mass-produced labels. These regional brew houses typically offer informative tours that are quite fun. Lew Bryson and Mark Haynie have written a very informative 2008 travel guide for all of Jersey's breweries and brewpubs. It is called *New Jersey Breweries* and I recommend it for anyone who enjoys a good beer run.

We visited most of these breweries and found a few similarities. The owners are passionate about their craft, and they are driven to create distinctive beers. All of them are focused on freshness and believe that their brews are far superior to the national brands.

The current trend for "green" products favors the microbreweries in that they typically buy, produce, and sell *locally*. They even recycle their used malted grain by selling or donating it to local farmers to feed livestock. Other than Budweiser produced in Newark, beer from the large national brands is made thousands of miles away, and then shipped in trucks, trains, and ships. This shipping not only affects the beer, but it creates a large environmental footprint. Unlike the national brands, local microbrews are not pasteurized so less energy is used in the bottling process.

New Jersey residents have been inundated with commercials for the mega-breweries, so most people associate beer with Bud or Coors. They buy beer without even considering smaller brands. The challenge for microbreweries is simply to get the public to try their beers. People who try the local beer generally will buy it again. An effective marketing technique would be to offer small samples in liquor stores, the way wine-makers often do. For reasons unknown, however, New Jersey law prohibits breweries from offering free beer sample in liquor stores. Similarly, wineries are permitted to sell an unlimited amount of wine right from their own winery, while New Jersey's breweries are limited to selling just one twelve-pack per customer.

Despite these disadvantages, the distinct flavors and quality offered by microbreweries have become more and more popular. According to the Brewers Association, craft brands are the fastest growing segment of beers. For example, in 2008, sales by small independent brands grew by over 7 percent while the major brands suffered a decrease in sales.

CLIMAX BREWING

The renaissance of Jersey beer began in 1994 when Climax Brewing was formed—although it did not begin selling beer until February of 1996. Located in Roselle Park at 112 Valley Road, Climax is now the oldest microbrewery in New Jersey. The owner, David Hoffman, was born and raised in Union County, and acquired his love for artisan beer from his father, Kurt, who was born in Germany. Once Dave started drinking his father's flavorful German imported beers, he could not drink the mass-marketed American style beers. David started with a home brew shop and confirmed the demand for small-batch, European style beer. Dave explains that North Jersey is great place to brew beer because of the water quality. "If the water is too hard then it is no good for lagers. If it's too soft then it is no good for ales. Our water is perfect for all styles."

With ten years of homebrewing experience, two years of professional consulting for Gold Coast Brewing Company, and owning his own homebrew supply store, Dave Hoffmann is firmly established in New Jersey's fastest-growing and newly emerging market. As head brewer, Dave has an extensive background in brewing, and formulated such beers as the well-acclaimed Hoboken Ale which is currently available throughout the northeast. He is also founder of "The Hanson House Hoppers," a Union County-based homebrew club, and has two entries in the book *Fifty Great Homebrew Tips*.

Climax offers a wide variety of ales and lagers under the labels Climax and Hoffman, and it handles its own distribution to ensure hands-on service throughout the State. You won't find typical bottles or cans of Dave's beer. Climax only sells its brews in half gallon "growlers" and kegs. Dave was initially disappointed that bottle manufacturers only made the half-gallon growlers in clear glass—which would allow light to damage the beer. After a few weeks of calls he was able to convince the largest bottle-maker to produce the jugs in brown glass. Dave also designed and built a custom filling machine to fill Climax's over-sized bottles.

Its styles are far from the mass-marketed lagers like Bud and Coors. By running a homebrew supply store, Dave had access to every type of ingredient and he learned how each ingredient added flavor to the

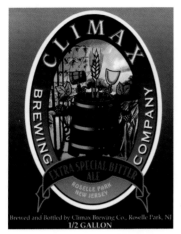

Climax's "Extra Special Bitter" label.

Hoffman lager by Climax.

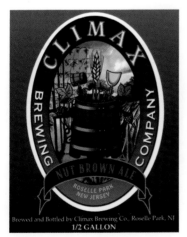

Nut Brown ale.

beer. "I felt traditional, full-bodied beers had been around for centuries for a reason, so I decided to brew those." Climax's first beer was an ESB (Extra Special Bitter style) which is very flavorful with a warm, spicy bitterness. Climax now offers a wide variety of seasonal and specialty beers including a porter, an India pale ale (IPA), a nut brown Ale and an Oktoberfest for fall. Climax's ESB was recognized in Michael Jackson's book, *Ultimate Beer*, as one of the best beers in the world. (Jackson's book is considered to be the "bible" of the beer-tasting world.) Based on this and several other positive reviews, Climax's sales continue to climb. It sells about 750 barrels per year and has capacity to expand to 4,000 barrels.

Climax's highly acclaimed
ESB growler bottle.

Climax Brewing Company
112 Valley Road
Roselle Park,
NJ 07204
www.climaxbrewing.com

CRICKET HILL BREWING COMPANY

Located at 24 Kulick Road in Fairfield, Cricket Hill Brewing opened in 2000 and offers a selection of beers in the middle ground between the Bud/Coors/Miller mass-produced beer and the stronger, hoppy European brews. Not too strong, not too weak, Cricket Hill aims to be "just right."

Cricket Hill produces about 1,000 barrels per year. Among its offerings is a unique Jersey Summer Breakfast Ale which is an unfiltered light ale with a hint of banana which is generated from the type of yeast used. Cricket Hill drinkers show their appreciation and loyalty by volunteering to assist with bottling on Thursday afternoons. Over twenty people typically attend these events and have a great time

Climax ad.

learning about brewing beer, socializing, and of course sampling some
fresh product.

Every Friday, brew master Rick Reed opens his doors to the public
for a free tasting tour of the brewery. Over 100 people typically attend
the Friday evening parties which include a passionate presentation
on the difference between mass-produced beer and local craft beer.
Reed's fiery speech has become legendary among fans of microbrews
and can been seen on www.youtube.com. Rick Reed is big on the
freshness of his brews. "If you like corn with your dinner" he explains,
"would you want to be served corn that was grown across the country,
pasteurized, canned, and shipped 1,000 miles? Or would you prefer
a fresh ear of Jersey corn that is seasoned and cooked in your home?
Cricket Hill's lagers and ales are fresh, flavorful, and brewed right here
in New Jersey."

Cricket Hill Summer *Breakfast* Ale. John Adams, who reportedly drank
a pint of porter beer with breakfast every morning, would be proud.

Cricket Hill Brewing Company, Inc.
24 Kulick Road
Fairfield, NJ 07004
www.crickethillbrewery.com

FLYING FISH BREWING COMPANY
"PROUDLY BREWED IN NEW JERSEY. YOU GOT A PROBLEM WITH THAT?"

Flying Fish brewery is the biggest Jersey brewer. Anheuser-Busch produces more beer at its Newark plant, but it is really a Missouri brewer. Gene Muller, the founder of Flying Fish, was working in advertising and had been homebrewing since 1980. He saw an opportunity to fill a niche market, and knew how to market it. He came up with a catchy brand name and logo, and started to promote the brand on the internet in 1995—before the brewery even existed. The brewery began production in August, 1996 at 1940 Olney Avenue in Cherry Hill.

The Cricket Hill family of beers.

Flying Fish offers a variety of ale styles including, Belgian Abbey Dubbel, HopFish IPA, ESB (English special bitter) Ale, XPA (Extra pale ale), and a variety of seasonals. The key word to describe all Flying Fish beers is "balance." The beers are full-flavored, yet highly drinkable.

Flying Fish is riding the trend for local products. It distributes to Pennsylvania, Maryland, and Delaware, but 85 percent of sales are within 100 miles of the brewery. The founder's background in marketing has paid off with some of the best labels, shirts, and slogans. Free tours are offered every Saturday from 1:00 to 4:00 p.m.

Flying Fish is kicking off a creative salute to New Jersey which it calls "The Exit Series"™ of beers. Over the next several years, they will create brews which reflect and celebrate the local flavor of each of New Jersey's exits. (For legal reasons, the brewery is careful not to specifically refer to the Turnpike or any specific highway.) Its first two releases salute Exit 4 with an American Triple ale in the Belgian style, and Exit 11 with a Hoppy American Wheat ale. Visit www.flyingfish.com to suggest a beer style which reflects your favorite exit.

A sampling of Flying Fish bottles.

Flying Fish Brewing Company
1940 Olney Avenue
Cherry Hill, NJ 08003
www.flyingfish.com

HIGH POINT BREWING COMPANY: RAMSTEIN

Founded in 1994, the High Point Brewing Company was the first brewery in America to exclusively brew wheat beer. They started with wheat ales, and have recently rolled out a few lagers without wheat. All of their brews are based on Old-World German tradition. The founder sought to locate the brewery near High Point in Wantage which is the highest point in New Jersey because the mountain terrain is similar to Bavaria. He wound up settling a bit farther south at 22 Park Place in Butler, but he kept the name High Point. The location in Butler was ideal because it is located on a natural spring-fed reservoir with soft water similar to the water used to make beer in the German mountains.

Greg Zaccardi founded High Point after winning awards as a home brewer. He learned his craft in southern Germany, and returned to America to produce Ramstein beers with ingredients (wheat, barley,

High Point's Blonde Wheat and
Classic Wheat beers.

hops, and yeast) imported directly from Bavaria, Germany. High Point
has exclusive rights to use a special yeast developed by a small brewery
in Bavaria. Other than the natural spring water, all of High Point's
ingredients are imported from Germany. After spending his college
years in California, Greg returned to New Jersey with a degree in
chemistry, and he was disappointed by the lack of variety offered by the
big national breweries. "My goal has been to bring traditional German
styles to America. I thought that the best application of my chemistry
degree would be to make beer."

High Point's beers have won many awards. Its Blonde Wheat won
the Gold Medal Best of Show in the 2001. *Mathew Vassar Cup* and Simon
& Schuster's *Pocket Guide to Beer* rates High Point's Dunkelweiss beer
the best of its kind in the world. Authentic German style beer seems to
be gaining popularity. Greg reports that sales and profits are rising.

Tours are available on the second Saturday of each month except
for January and February.

High Point's "Ramstein Classic Wheat Beer" label.

High Point Brewing Company, Inc.
22 Park Place
Butler, New Jersey 07405
www.ramsteinbeer.com

RIVER HORSE BREWING COMPANY

River Horse was founded in 1996 by three brothers, Jim, Jack, and Tim Bryan at 80 Lambert Lane in Lambertville, along the bank of the Delaware River. The Bryan brothers sold to a new group in 2006. Production is about 4,500 barrels per year in a variety of styles including lager, Hop Hazard Pale Ale, Special Ale ESB, Summer Blonde Ale, Belgian Frostbite Winter Ale, and Triplehorse (10 percent alcohol by volume—which they claim improves with age). River Horse uses only natural ingredients and local Jersey spring water. Tours and samples are offered every Friday through Sunday, starting at noon.

Six-pack of River Horse Belgian style ale.

River Horse Brewing Company
80 Lambert Lane
Lambertville, NJ 08530
www.riverhorse.com

BREW PUBS

The Ship Inn Restaurant and Brewery was the first brew pub to open under a 1994 law that allowed brew pubs to open in New Jersey. Wasting no time, it opened in January 1995 in Milford, New Jersey.

Triumph Brewing Company of Princeton was the second to open in March 1995, and the Long Valley Pub and Brewery followed soon after in Morris County.

Probably the most well-known brew pub in New Jersey, is Basil T's Brewpub and Italian Grill located at 183 Riverside Avenue in Red Bank. They offer six handcrafted beers (including a seasonal beer) by the pint, mug, growler, or sampler. Their stout has won several awards.

There are way too many brew pubs around the State to list them all. Most have thrived by offering good food and distinctive beers.

For those who'd like to try their hand at creating their very own *Jersey Brew*, the Brewer's Apprentice in Freehold makes it easy. Just choose from their extensive list of recipes (or create your own) and they provide all of the ingredients, equipment, bottles, labels, and advice to make your own beer.

BEER BREAK: *BEER PROBLEMS AND SOLUTIONS*

PROBLEM: Feet cold and wet.
CAUSE: Glass being held at incorrect angle.
SOLUTION: Rotate glass so that open end points toward ceiling.

PROBLEM: Beer unusually pale and tasteless.
CAUSE: Glass empty.
SOLUTION: Get someone to buy you another beer.

PROBLEM: Beer tasteless, front of your shirt is wet.
CAUSE: Mouth not open, or glass applied to wrong part of face.
SOLUTION: Retire to restroom, practice in mirror.

PROBLEM: Floor blurred.
CAUSE: You are looking through bottom of empty glass.
SOLUTION: Get someone to buy you another beer.

PROBLEM: Floor moving.
CAUSE: You are being carried out.
SOLUTION: Find out if you are being taken to another bar.

PROBLEM: Everyone looks up to you and smiles.
CAUSE: You are dancing on the table.
SOLUTION: Fall on somebody cushy-looking.

PROBLEM: Beer is crystal-clear.
CAUSE: It's water. Somebody is trying to sober you up.
SOLUTION: Punch him.

PROBLEM: Hands hurt, nose hurts, mind unusually clear.
CAUSE: You have been in a fight.
SOLUTION: Apologize to everyone you see, just in case it was them.

Source: Unknown author

10 | New Jersey Beer Association

www.njbeer.org

The Garden State Craft Brewers Guild

About the Guild

The Garden State Craft Brewers Guild is an association of the restricted and limited license holders in New Jersey. Our goal is to promote the craft brewing industry in New Jersey by means of education, promotion of special events and other social, civic and economic initiatives.

Reprinted with permission of the Garden State Craft Brewers Guild.

Locator Map for Member Breweries

1 Red Bank
1 Toms River
2 Vineland
3 Cherry Hill
4 South Orange
5 New Brunswick
6 Ocean Township
7 Butler
8 Woodbridge
9 Sparta
10 Long Valley
11 Metuchen
12 Lambertville
13 Milford
14 Berkeley Heights
15 Princeton
16 Atlantic City

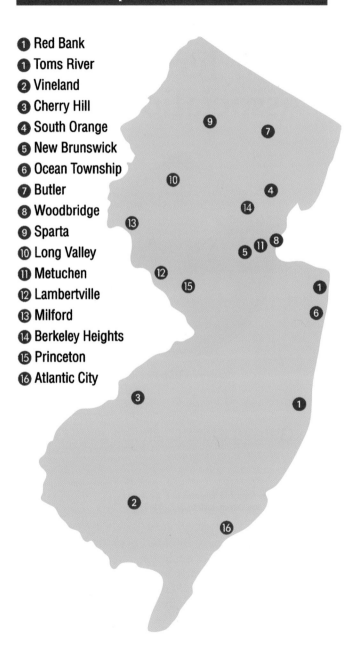

Please support the members of the
Garden State Craft Brewers Guild:

❶ Basil T's Brew Pub & Italian Grill
183 Riverside Avenue, Red Bank, NJ 07701
(732) 842-5990   www.basilt.com
1171 Hooper Avenue, Toms River, NJ 08753
(732) 244-7566   www.basilt.com

❷ Blue Collar Brewing Company
1200 S.W.Boulevard, Vineland, NJ 08360
(856) 690 1950   www.bluecollarbrewing.com

❸ Flying Fish Brewing Company
18 Olney Avenue, Cherry Hill, NJ 08003
(856) 489-0061   www.flyingfish.com

❹ Gaslight Brewery & Restaurant
15 South Orange Avenue, South Orange, NJ 07079
(973) 762-7077   www.gaslightbrewery.com

❺ Harvest Moon Brewery and Café
392 George Street, New Brunswick, NJ 08901
(732) 249-6666

❻ Heavyweight Brewing Company
1701 Valley Road, Ocean Township, NJ 07712
(732) 493-5009   www.heavyweight-brewing.com

❼ High Point Wheat Beer Company
22 Park Place, Butler NJ 07405
(973) 838-7400   www.ramsteinbeer.com

❽ J.J.Bitting Brewing Company
33 Main Street, Woodbridge, NJ 07095
(732) 634-2929   www.njbrewpubs.com

❾ Krogh's Restaurant & Brew Pub
23 White Deer Plaza, Sparta, NJ 07871
(973) 729-8428   www.kroghs.com

❿ Long Valley Pub and Brewery
Routes 513/24 & 517, Long Valley, NJ 07853
(908) 876-1122

⓫ Pizzeria Uno Chicago Grill & Brewery
61 U.S. Highway #1, Metuchen, NJ 08840
(732) 548-7979   www.pizzeriauno.com

⓬ River Horse Brewing Company
80 Lambert Lane, Lambertville, NJ 08530
(609) 397-7776   www.riverhorse.com

⓭ The Ship Inn Restaurant & Brewery
61 Bridge Street, Milford, NJ 08848
1-800-NJ1-ALES   www.shipinn.com

⓮ Trap Rock Restaurant & Brewery
279 Springfield Avenue, Berkeley Heights, NJ 07922
(908) 665-1755

⓯ Triumph Brewing Company
138 Nassau Street, Princeton, NJ 08542
(609) 924-7855   www.triumphbrew.com

⓰ Tun Tavern Brewery & Restaurant
2000 Kirkman Boulevard, Atlantic City, NJ 08401
(609) 347-7800   www.tuntavern.com

① *Basil T's*
Brew Pub & Italian Grill

Basil T's Brew Pub & Italian Grill – Brewpub

183 Riverside Avenue, Red Bank, NJ 07701
(732) 842-5990   **www.basilt.com**
1171 Hooper Avenue, Toms River, NJ 08753
(732) 244-7566   **www.basilt.com**

New Jersey's first and only brewpub with two locations,
Basil T's is an elegant full-service restaurant serving
authentic gourmet Italian specialties as well as Pizza
Vera Napolitana and burgers. There are always at
least six hand-crafted ales on tap, and both locations
include a members-only cigar lounge. The bar features
New Jersey's largest mug club, happy hour, and live
music on Wednesday through Saturday evenings.

②

Blue Collar Brewing Company – Microbrewery

1200 S.W. Boulevard, Vineland, NJ 08360
(856) 690-1950   www.bluecollarbrewing.com

Blue Collar is southern New Jersey's newest
microbrewery, having opened in October 1999. B.C.B.
produces five ales and three seasonal lagers in both
American and German styles. Recently B.C.B. began
bottling their brews in quarts and pints, which are
available in area liquor stores and fine restaurants.
Call ahead for tour and tasting info.

Flying Fish Brewing Company – Microbrewery

18 Olney Avenue, Cherry Hill, NJ 08003
(856) 489-0061 **www.flyingfish.com**

Flying Fish is the first microbrewery in the southern half of New Jersey and the most widely produced craft beer in the state. We specialize in classic English and Belgian styles and currently produce five bottled products: ESB Ale, Extra Pale Ale, Porter, Belgian Abbey Dubbel, and Farmhouse Summer Ale. In addition, we brew a variety of draft-only seasonals and cask-conditioned "real ales." Flying Fish was a Gold medal winner at the 2000 U.S. Real Ale Festival.

Gaslight Brewery & Restaurant – Brewpub

15 South Orange Ave, South Orange, NJ 07079
(973) 762-7077 **www.gaslightbrewery.com**

This is Essex County's first brewpub. We offer a relaxed atmosphere where people can come to enjoy freshly brewed beer and delicious food, watch a game on TV, play darts or shuffleboard, and listen to good music. We try to make this a spot where everyone can have some fun. We try to have live entertainment at least three times a week.

Harvest Moon Brewery and Café – Brewpub

392 George Street, New Brunswick, NJ 08901
(732) 249-6666

The Harvest Moon Brewery and Café is a casual relaxed restaurant offering creative American cuisine at affordable prices in a unique setting serving lunch, dinner, late night food, and an à la carte Sunday Brunch. Handcrafted freshly brewed English style ales including our flagship brews, seasonal, cask-conditioned, dry hopped, and guest taps are served at New Brunswick's biggest bar with a great happy hour and outstanding live entertainment nightly. We also offer a fine selection of premium cigars.

Heavyweight Brewing Company – Microbrewery

1701 Valley Road, Ocean Township, NJ 07712
(732) 493-5009   www.heavyweight-brewing.com

Heavyweight specializes in making bold beers in our small brewery in Ocean Township. We are dedicated to producing interesting beers of distinction and quality for the discriminating beer drinker. Our philosophy is simple. There are many great pale and amber ales; we prefer instead to brew those interesting and hard to find styles. You can find our products in bottle and on draft in New Jersey and Pennsylvania—bigger and smaller than most.

High Point Wheat Beer Company – Microbrewery

22 Park Place, Butler, NJ 07405
(973) 838-7400   **www.ramsteinbeer.com**

High Point Wheat Beer Company is the first exclusive wheat beer brewery in America. High Point brews the award-winning Ramstein beers. Ramstein beers are available on draft and in bottles throughout New Jersey, New York, and Pennsylvania. High Point's brewery is in Butler, New Jersey. Free brewery tours are held on the second Saturday of each month from 2-4 p.m. Please visit www.ramsteinbeer.com for more information.

J.J. Bitting Brewing Company – Brewpub

33 Main Street, Woodbridge, NJ 07095
(732) 634-2929   **www.njbrewpubs.com**

J.J. Bitting Brewing Co. is located in a turn of the century coal and grain depot in downtown Woodbridge. We offer up to six handcrafted brews plus a cask-conditioned ale on our authentic hand pump, along with award-winning American grill cuisine. Private parties, outdoor deck, and central New Jersey's best happy hour are just a few of the reasons to come and join the fun.

Krogh's Restaurant & Brew Pub – Brewpub

23 White Deer Plaza, Sparta, NJ 07871
(973) 729-8428   www.kroghs.com

At Krogh's Restaurant & Brew Pub, we feature seven handcrafted beers brewed onsite. Our extensive lunch and dinner menu has everything from burgers to pasta and Mexican to Cajun. Krogh's is "the" spot in Sussex county with the best regional and national acts performing four nights a week. For a complete menu and music calendar, visit our Web site at www.kroghs.com.

Long Valley Pub and Brewery – Brewpub

Routes 513/24 & 517, Long Valley, NJ 07853
(908) 876-1122

Long Valley Pub and Brewery is a 7-barrel brewpub housed in a completely restored 250+ year-old stone barn. Featuring two bars, a diverse menu, and a broad range of beer styles, the pub also features seasonal outdoor dining. It was winner of the 1999 Great American Beer Festival bronze medal for Robust Porter.

Pizzeria Uno Chicago Grill & Brewery – Brewpub

61 U.S. Highway #1, Metuchen, NJ 08840
(732) 548-7979   www.pizzeriauno.com

We've evolved the Pizzeria Uno legend to a brewhouse as well. Our Brewmaster, Mike Sella, brews all of our own beer on premise, using a custom-built 15-barrel pub brewing system. Mike has formulated these beers to be the perfect complement to our delicious food. Fresh beer tastes best.

River Horse Brewing Company – Microbrewery

80 Lambert Lane, Lambertville, NJ 08530
(609) 397-7776   www.riverhorse.com

River Horse is a 20-barrel microbrewery located on the Delaware River in Hunterdon County. Opened in April 1996, the brewery produces both ales and lagers and currently features five products. River Horse has an attractive gift shop and is open for both tours and tastings seven days a week, from noon to 4 p.m.

The Ship Inn Restaurant & Brewery – Brewpub

61 Bridge Street, Milford, NJ 08848
1-800-NJ1-ALES   **www.shipinn.com**

The Ship Inn is an English pub set in the scenic Delaware River valley. It specializes in British and Continental cuisine, single malt whiskeys, ports, imported British beer, and of course, its own traditional cask-conditioned ales brewed on the premises.

Trap Rock Restaurant & Brewery – Brewpub

279 Springfield Avenue, Berkeley Heights, NJ 07922
(908) 665-1755

In early April 1997, Trap Rock opened its doors. Not your typical brewpub, these doors allow you to walk into a world that makes you feel comfortable in an English country inn setting without leaving North-Central New Jersey. Trap Rock offers a blend of classical American/French cuisine, exceptional beer styles, and impeccable service.

Triumph Brewing Company – Brewpub

138 Nassau Street, Princeton, NJ 08542
(609) 924-7855   www.triumphbrew.com

An ambitious and eclectic menu is served in an architecturally unique setting. Seven craft-brewed beers are always on tap including ales, lagers, nitro-pour stout, and hand-pumped real ale.

Tun Tavern Brewery & Restaurant – Brewpub

2000 Kirkman Boulevard, Atlantic City, NJ 08401
(609) 347-7800   www.tuntavern.com

Tun Tavern is Atlantic City's first and only brewpub. It was recently voted the Number One Restaurant in New Jersey by the *Server Foodservice News* and Favorite Brewpub in New Jersey by readers of Gary Monterosso's *What's on Tap* newsletter. Tun Tavern offers casual gourmet cuisine, handcrafted brews, and live entertainment seven days per week including live reggae music on the outdoor deck every Sunday at 4 p.m. in the summer. Parking is free on Michigan Avenue.

BEER BREAK: *JERSEY BREW RESOURCES*

If you like what you have read here and would like to read more
about the current state of beer in New Jersey, there are plenty of
resources. Visit one of the five local craft breweries for a tour and
sampling, spend some time at a brew pub, and check out these
newsletters, blogs and websites for beer lovers:

www.alestreetnews.com
www.bcca.com
www.beerstainedletter.blogspot.com
www.beeradvocate.com
www.beertravelers.com
www.beerme.com
www.breweriana.com
www.brucemobley.com
www.conetops.com
www.lewbryson.com
www.njbeer.org
www.pubcrawler.com
www.realbeer.com
www.taverntrove.com

11 | Last Call

THE UNEXAMINED BEER IS NOT WORTH DRINKING

Most people enjoy beer without giving it much thought, and there is nothing wrong with that. I followed that road for a long time. I've never been to a formal beer tasting. I mainly drank Bud for the first few years of my adult life. My interest in New Jersey's history gradually led me to the history of beer, and that led me to a greater appreciation for beer and its many different styles. I hope that this book has opened this same door for the reader.

Socrates is often quoted for saying "the unexamined life is not worth living." I wouldn't go quite so far as to say this about beer, because most beer is good whether you think about it or not. But, like most things, a deeper understanding of beer leads to a deeper level of enjoyment.

I hope you enjoyed this book and I hope it has encouraged you to try a few different brands and ask your local store to stock beer from a few of New Jersey's microbreweries.

Campaign for New Jersey beer.

About the Author

MICHAEL PELLEGRINO IS AN ATTORNEY WITH OFFICES IN DENVILLE AND Westwood, New Jersey. He graduated from Rutgers Law School in 1991 and is a former elected councilman in Westwood. Mike is the author of two other books, *Westwood, Postcard History* and *Tax Lien$, The Complete Guide to Investing in New Jersey Tax Liens*. He supports the local microbreweries and loves to hunt down and try a new brew.

Resources

1. Tapping a Jersey Brew

2. The Importance of Beer in Early America
- *100 Years of Brewing* (New York and Chicago: H.S. Rich & Company, 1903).
- Wood, William. *New England Prospects* (Boston, Mass., np 1635, pg. 55 as quoted in *Beer in America, The Early Years*.

3. New Jersey's Earliest Breweries
- www.balantine.com
- Beer Can Collectors of America. *United States Beer Cans* (Beer Can Collectors of America: Fenton, Mo).
- "Creative Specifications Essential for Advertising Success." *Modern Brewery Age*. October 1954.
- Dikun, John. "Gottfried Krueger Brewing Company." *American Breweriana Journal*.
- "Krueger Introduces Canned Beer." *Modern Brewery*. March 1935.
- "Men Who You Know." *Modern Brewery*. September 15, 1933.
- Pawlowski, Steve. "The G. Krueger Brewing Company." *BCCA News Report* (March – April 1985), pg. 5–7.
- "The 'K' Man." *Modern Brewer*. September 1937.

- "$1,000,000 In Beer Spilled Into Sewer: Brewery's 16-Year-Old Product Drained After Vain Efforts to Dispose of It Legally." *New York Times*, November 1, 1927.
- "Feigenspan Quits as Brewers' Chief: Says He Opposes Any Negotiating With Anti-Salon League Officials." *New York Times*, September 24, 1925.
- www.newarkhistory.com/colleoni
- Various articles on Peter Breidt in *New York Times*, including October 19, 1923; October 21, 1923; December 4, 1923; and September 1, 1926.
- "Orange Brewery History," supplied by Scott Walker: http://freepages.history.rootsweb.ancestry.com/~orangebrew/index.htm
- www.beercans.org
- www.beercannews.com
- www.njbeer.org
- www.beernexis.com
- Will Anderson, *The Beer Poster Book*, 1976.
- Weiss, Harry B., and Grace M. Weiss. *The Early Breweries of New Jersey*, 1963.
- Salem, F.W. Beer, *Its History and Its Economic Value as a National Beverage* (1880).
- *New York Times*: December 9, 1889; December 3, 1889; October 21, 1948, April 8, 1949; April 14, 1949; and April 15, 1949.

4. The Bishops' Law
- Paulsson, Martin. *The Social Anxieties of Progressive Reform, Atlantic City* 1854–1920.

5. Prohibition Years
- Stuart, Mark A. *Gangster #2, Longy Zwillman*.
- Reeves, Col. Ira. *Ole Rum River*.

6. New Jersey's Beer Mob
- Tomlinson, Gerald. *Murdered in New Jersey*.
- Blackwell, Jon. *Notorious New Jersey*.

- Taggert, Ed. *Bootlegger: Max Hassel, The Millionaire Newsboy.*
- Stewart, Mark A. *Gangster # 2: Longy Zwillman.*
- Tomlinson, Gerald. *Murdered in New Jersey.*
- Block, Alan. *East Side – West Side, Organizing Crime in New York.*
- Fried, Albert. *The Rise and Fall of the Jewish Gangster in America.*
- Eisenberg, Dennis. *Meyer Lansky: Mogul of the Mob.*
- Blackwell, Jon. *Notorious New Jersey.*
- Taggert, Edward. "Beer Baron Max Hassel," the *Historical Review of Berks County.* Historical Society of Berks County. Summer edition.

7. The Beer Can—a Jersey Invention

- "Creative Specifications Essential for Advertising Success." *Modern Brewery Age.* October 1954.
- Dikun, John. "Gottfried Krueger Brewing Company." *American Breweriana Journal.*
- "Krueger Introduces Canned Beer." *Modern Brewery.* March 1935.
- "Men Who You Know." *Modern Brewery.* September 15, 1933.
- "The G. Krueger Brewing Company" *BCCA News Report* (March–April 1985), pg. 5–7.

8. Types of Jersey Beer

9. Resurgence of Jersey Brewers: Micro Breweries

- Personal visits to breweries.
- Garden State Craft Brewers Guild.
- Bryson, Lew, and Mark Haynie, *New Jersey Breweries* (2008).

10. New Jersey Beer Association

- www.njbeer.org